FOREIGN
LANGUAGE
INSTRUCTION

FOREIGN LANGUAGE INSTRUCTION

Dimensions and Horizons

Ruth R. Cornfield

Ph.D., Communications in Education

New York

APPLETON-CENTURY-CROFTS

Division of Meredith Publishing Company

PREFACE

This book was written for those who are interested in the teaching of foreign languages—the student preparing for the profession and the teacher already in the classroom. *Foreign Language Instruction: Dimensions and Horizons* grew out of the need for a comprehensive, useful text on new methods for teaching foreign languages which could be used in many kinds of teaching situations with various types of teaching materials, the old and the new.

The practices and procedures one uses, however, are determined by the objectives to be achieved. Obviously today's world demands that people perform in all the language skills. The direction in which one is headed determines the choice of roads to be traveled. The classroom techniques which the teacher selects, regardless of the materials used, must result in performance by the student.

Responding to the request for practical, feasible ideas, the techniques described in this book were included only after each had been tested in a variety of classroom situations. The methods of instruction covered in this text do not pertain to any one course or any one set of materials. They are adaptable for use with all of them; from the traditional textbook to the audio-visual-lingual programs.

This book was planned to give help, instruction, and information to all who seek it; to the novice, anxious for suggestions in planning his lessons and presenting them in front of a class and to the experienced teacher who wants to learn new tricks and yet needs to be reminded of some of the old ones which he may have forgotten.

Although *Foreign Language Instruction: Dimensions and Horizons* is intended for the teacher, it is written with the learner uppermost in mind. The practices which are discussed in this book are aimed at providing him with satisfactory and pleasurable experiences. Learning a foreign language can and should be fun.

In my desire to provide as complete a text as possible, I have delved into the recesses of my mind as well as the recesses of the library. I trust that I have given proper credit to the originators of the ideas which I have culled from all sources. No book is written without incurring an indebtedness to many people. I am grateful to them all, those to whom I can give credit and to the many others who have shaped my thinking without their names having been impressed on my consciousness.

Those without whose help I could never have achieved this book and whose assistance I gratefully acknowledge are my dear friend and teacher, Dr. Irene F. Cypher, Professor of Communications in Education at New York University, who took many precious hours from her myriad pressing personal and professional duties to read and examine the manuscript; Mrs. Lorna Prince of West Philadelphia High School who looked at what I was writing with the critical, quizzical eye and mind of a teacher in the classroom; Dr. Helen Burchell of the University of Pennsylvania; SWC, my severest critic; those teachers and student-teachers whom I observed as they were testing old and new procedures with their classes; and the students in my courses on whom I tried my ideas before putting them down on paper.

To Dr. Edgar Dale of Ohio State University I take this occasion to acknowledge with gratitude all the inspiration, philosophy, and ideas given me through his valuable publications.

To all these I say, "Thank you."

                                                                R.R.C.

CONTENTS

1
INTRODUCTION—
WHY WE ARE TEACHING
FOREIGN LANGUAGES

- *For World Understanding*

  It is often necessary to be able to understand and speak the languages of those from other countries in order to create a warm, sustaining relationship with them.

- *For Use in Commerce and Industry*

  Since thousands of Americans desire employment abroad, it is wise for the student to prepare himself today for those opportunities of tomorrow.

- *For Travel*

  The tourist who knows how to communicate with the native population profits most from his trip, socially as well as economically.

- *For Pleasure*

  The study of foreign languages offers one leisure-time activities for a lifetime of pleasure.

- *For Insight Into One's Own Language*

  The knowledge of a second language stimulates an awareness and curiosity about the structure and rationale of one's own language.

Never before in the history of the world has the need been so great for communication among peoples of many tongues. Never before has the study of foreign languages been as necessary as it is today. The public is becoming increasingly curious and interested and many questions are being asked about foreign language instruction. These questions come from many quarters: the student, the parent, the school board, the principal, the superintendent, the PTA, and even the college and the university. Often the introduction of the study of foreign languages into a school or a school system depends on how well these questions are answered by those who are engaged in teaching in this area.

The student and the parent who are concerned about entrance into college will unfortunately be satisfied with an answer if it includes the promise that the necessary requirements will be fulfilled. If several years of foreign language study will prepare the student for nothing more than passing one college entrance examination, it is indeed a very high price for the student and the community to pay in time and money.

Actually other more valid reasons justify spending school time in the study of foreign languages and the student who is deriving all there is to derive from his efforts in this endeavor will not only be able to pass any examination which comes his way but will also have acquired other much more valuable and lasting assets.

FOR USE IN WORLD UNDERSTANDING

Obviously no longer is any ocean wide enough or any mountain high enough to separate the nations of this earth from each other. Daily events in all parts of the world make all of us uncomfortably aware that it is not a matter of choice but a necessity to get along with our neighbors. What better way is there to understand him than to meet him face to face and to speak to him in his own language? To comprehend the culture from which his language grows, the customs from which his activities emanate, and the history upon which his civilization is built is to really comprehend *him,* for all of these influence his thoughts and the meaning of the words he utters.

The better we understand his background, environment, and the stimuli to which he reacts, the firmer become the lines of communication between us. Concepts and thoughts, not words, are what we require for communication. Effective understanding can take place only where both sender and receiver utter the same organized system of sounds and have accumulated the same concepts for these sounds. Such interaction cannot be accomplished through a translator or an interpreter, for he is more concerned with words than with concepts. For example, the Eskimo, the South Sea Islander, and the Tibetan live in very different kinds of dwellings. The translation of the names of these various structures into the word "house" cannot convey the real concept of each of these very dissimilar abodes.

No longer is it only the diplomat and the high government official who are responsible for international understanding. The clerks and secretaries who work in foreign branch offices, the wives and families of the armed forces, the exchange students, and the Peace Corps workers are all ambassadors without portfolio and represent their government wherever they go. These people who come into daily contact with the native population are actually more important for establishing world understanding than the government official who is not likely to have the opportunity to mingle at the grass roots level. The need for comprehending the concepts behind the spoken word in the streets, in the homes, in the offices, and in the shops is very obvious. Numerous stories have been told of fiascoes which have resulted in bitter feelings because of the misinterpretation of gestures and sounds or the ignorance of customs and taboos by groups of people who had been sent to live in a part of the world whose language they did not speak.

Has not the tourist also the responsibility for fostering international understanding when he travels to other parts of the world? A monolingual American, like any other tourist, is bound to be circumscribed by the one language he speaks and the culture and way of life it represents. Such provincialism will certainly be lessened by the study of a second language. Gaining insight into another culture tends to make one more tolerant and less critical of those who have different standards of living. The tourist who travels in foreign lands and speaks foreign languages is in a position to make many friends for himself and his country.

FOR USE IN COMMERCE AND INDUSTRY

There are millions of Americans who work abroad and the number is increasing each year according to the United States Department of Commerce statistics. Industry is no longer considered a nation-wide activity circumscribed by our own borders. We all know that business sees the world as its marketplace and that almost every large corporation is making an effort to capture its share of the world's income. Smaller enterprises, too, are no longer content to be limited by the borders of this continent for their merchandising pursuits. Many are opening branch offices, centers, and factories essential to carrying on business all over the world. The members of the staff in these offices must, of necessity, be able to converse in the language of the country to which they are assigned. The time to prepare for such opportunities is in school.

Study of one foreign language gives the student insight into other languages. Learning to perceive the structure, rationale, and applied linguistics of one language awakens one's perception about other languages.

The particular language which one chooses to study today may or may not be the one which will prove to be the most useful ten, twenty, or thirty years hence. It is not unreasonable to assume that a student who studies Spanish today may need to know one of the African or Asian languages some time in the future. No one can foresee what circumstances may arise in one's lifetime which will require the knowledge and the use of another language. Which foreign language it will be is certainly impossible to predict when one is in the fourth, seventh, or even the ninth grade.

Therefore, unless one has a very strong reason for preferring one language to another, the choice of which foreign language to study is relatively unimportant. What is important is that the student gain insight into the structure of the language he is studying so that he can intelligently apply that knowledge to the study of any other language, should the opportunity or need arise.

Such opportunities are constantly increasing. More and more people are called upon, by government and industry, to leave the United States without too much advance notice and to take up residence in the far-flung corners of the world. Those who know the nature and organization of language and have acquired the knowledge of at least one foreign language have, under normal circumstances, a better chance of being chosen for that overseas job than those who know no language but their own.

FOR USE IN TRAVEL

Happily, travel is no longer reserved for a small, select segment of our population. In this jet age one does not need very much time or money to indulge in this pleasurable pastime. The clerk, the secretary, the factory worker, the housewife, anyone in fact, with a few days of free time can travel anywhere on the face of this earth. There are few places farther away from the United States than twenty-four hours in flying time and tickets can be purchased on the installment plan if ready cash is not available.

However, too often the voyager discovers that traveling in a country where one cannot communicate with the waiter, the salesclerk, the taxi driver, and the hotel clerk can turn out to be a frustrating and very unrewarding experience. He is forced to seek out those who speak his own language. He may have to socialize only with his own compatriots and patronize a selected number of restaurants and shops, usually very expensive, which cater to people who have not learned to speak the language of the land. In fact, the monolingual traveler is cut off from that which he is spending his money to discover, interesting restaurants, the best bargains, or an insight into the way of life of a community. This he can best learn by direct contact with the people, by exchanging ideas with them, and by frequenting those places where the native population is to be found.

Certainly, the most colorful and rewarding way to explore a city is by public conveyance where one can mix with the crowd and get to the typically native out-of-the-way places. Half the fun of traveling in foreign lands is the joy of discovering the little restaurants and the indigenous foods in those interesting places which are off the beaten path and are known only to the local society. Here one's pleasure is definitely increased by the ability to understand the menu, and the opportunity to converse in the native language with the waiter, as well as with other people in the restaurant.

The great tourist sport of shopping is less enjoyable and without a doubt more costly unless one knows the native language and customs. To his dismay many a traveler discovers that in some lands a little haggling is expected to take place before a purchase is made. Even if he is aware of this fact, where communication is limited and inadequate he cannot indulge in such a pleasant adventure. It is obvious that the buyer who is at the mercy of the seller rarely makes the best deal. The bargain one can effect in the marketplace is remembered with pleasure for a long time.

FOR PLEASURE

No man can be considered educated who has not devoted some time to the development of activities which are purely cultural, enriching, and pleasure-giving and which help him to raise his sights and broaden his intellectual horizons. If his scholastic pursuits have been only vocational, be he carpenter or doctor, he has been trained, but not educated. To develop those skills and talents which will permit one to fill the leisure time with pleasure is becoming more and more of a necessity in our era. Retirement age is lower, working days are growing shorter, and free time is growing longer. The educated man is one who has many areas of interest to develop and enjoy.

The acquisition of a foreign language can contribute many hours of pleasure to one's leisure-time activities. Acquiring a foreign language is much like embarking on a trip to explore a foreign land, a trip which takes one into myriad areas and which continues throughout one's lifetime. The choice of what one wants to explore is limited only by one's imagination and ingenuity. The knowledge of a foreign language opens new avenues of absorbing inquiry and examination of various aspects of a foreign culture and civilization, such as the arts, sciences, and humanities.

Becoming involved in the acquisition of a foreign language helps to widen one's social activities. It is normal to seek out other people with similar interests in order to practice and perfect the use of that language. There is hardly a city or town which does not have its Alliance Française or Pan American Club where its membership is involved in various pleasurable pursuits connected with language learning. Art, music, and literature take on new dimensions as do handicrafts and artifacts.

Learning to appreciate a foreign culture develops the recognition and enjoyment of the attainments and accomplishments of the men of arts and sciences in one's own country.

FOR GREATER INSIGHT INTO ONE'S OWN LANGUAGE

Not the least among the previously cited advantages of becoming acquainted with another idiom is the insight that such a study gives one into one's own language. Recognition of word families, cognates, synonyms, and other linguistic phenomena in a foreign language stimulates an awareness of and a curiosity about one's own native vocabulary. Focusing attention on phraseology, choice of words, and modes of expression in another language carries over into one's native language. Learning to express ideas in a foreign language tends to make the student concentrate on the style of presentation. Seeking the nuance of the meaning of a foreign word or phrase makes one conscious of the shades of meaning implicit in the words and phrases of one's own language. Not only is vocabulary bound to grow, but also the habit of choosing the right word for the right idea is certain to result.

Knowledge of the structure of a foreign language usually makes one conscious of the structure of one's own word relationships and the role of words in sentences. Tenses, connecting words, and prepositions begin to be more meaningful. Proverbs, and colorful idiomatic expressions may make one inquire about similar cultural expressions in one's own language with the attendant explanations of how they are alike or different, and what lies behind the differences in imagery or structure.

Verbal perception, awareness, and experience must result in a better, more sensitive instrument for effective communication of thoughts and ideas in the native language.

SUGGESTED READINGS:

Department of Foreign Languages, "Should My Child Study a Foreign Language?" National Education Association, Washington, D.C. 20036.

Department of Health, Education, and Welfare, "A Partial List of Sources of Information Concerning Teaching Positions Outside the Continental Limits of the United States" (OE-14060-62), 1962, U.S. Department of Health, Education, and Welfare, Washington, D.C.

Department of State, "Career Opportunities as a Foreign Service Officer," Publication 7245, 1961, Superintendent of Documents, Washington, D.C.

Eaton, Esther, et al., "Source Materials for Secondary School Teachers of Foreign Languages," Bulletin 1962 (OE-27001B), U.S. Department of Health, Education, and Welfare, Office of Education, Washington, D.C. 20202.

Hall, Edward T., The Silent Language (Garden City, N.Y., Doubleday, 1959).

Johnston, Marjorie C., "Designing Foreign Language Education for World Understanding—A Shared Responsibility," General Meeting on Foreign Language Program, December 29, 1962, Department of Foreign Languages, National Education Association, Washington, D.C. 20036.

Remer, Ilo, "A Handbook for Guiding Students in Modern Foreign Languages," Bulletin 1963, No. 26 (OE-27018), U.S. Department of Health, Education, and Welfare, Office of Education, Washington, D.C. 20202.

Sumner, William G., Folkways (Boston, Ginn, 1940).

2
WHAT IS LANGUAGE?

- Language is an *oral* means of communication between people.
- Language teachers should know something about psychology, linguistics, and cultural anthropology in addition to the structure of the language they teach.
- There are problem areas which are peculiar to second language teaching.

DEFINITION

It is far more difficult to define the word language with precision than it is to define a scientific term or a concrete object. We are dealing with a phenomenon which is subtle, complex, and difficult to formulate. Therefore, before attempting a definition of what language is, it might help first to consider what language is not.

To many people language is conceived to be what is written in books, newspapers, letters, magazines, and the like. Only what is found in "black on white" is believed to be significant, truthful, and worthy of study and consideration. However, spoken language existed long before written symbols for language were invented. Even today almost half of the inhabitants of this earth cannot read or write, but they use language to conduct their social and economic affairs with great effectiveness. In Mexico and Central America alone, hundreds of tribes never devised a written language and over the many centuries have never found the need to develop one. This is also true of countless tribes in Africa.

The Mazateco tribe of Mexico has two oral languages, one which is spoken and one which is whistled. The whistled language duplicates the intonation patterns of the spoken language and is used between two widely-separated places because it carries better.

The Wycliffe Bible translators tell us that there are at least 2,000 tribes in the world whose languages have no written signs. These languages are only now being codified by linguists, so that written forms may result. One can therefore conclude that language is not what is written. That which is written is merely the symbol of language.

Some view language as that which is learned in school. There are teachers and students who consider language learning to be a thorough mastery of the grammatical rules of a language. Were this the case, children would not be able to speak correctly without learning rules of grammar. In many nations grammar books have never been written. Despite this fact, their populations speak highly inflected, intricate, and complex languages. On the other hand, there are myriads of students who can correctly give all the rules of grammar of a foreign language and recite all the functions of the parts of speech and yet are incapable of speaking that language. Charlton Laird in his book *The Miracle of Language* tells us that grammar is inherent in language, but is not language and cannot exist without language. Therefore, we can say that the study of a language is not synonymous with the study of its rules of grammar.

Translation is not the study of a language. It can even be an instrument through which language can become confused resulting in misconception and misinformation. This can be seen from the following example:

"Open your readers to page 10. Tom, will you begin to translate from the top of the page?" says the teacher who believes that translation is the study of language. The first sentence reads: *"La maman de Pierre va au magasin pour acheter du pain."* "Peter's mother goes to the store to buy some bread," translates Tom who is led to believe that what he and his class are doing is studying French.

What meaning do these English words convey to the student who translated a sentence which was written by a Frenchman who probably had no knowledge of English? What concept does the student translator have? Does this sentence mean what Tom knows about going to the store to buy bread? Did Pierre's mother hop into the car to go to the supermarket in the shopping center to get a loaf of cellophane-wrapped bread from the shelf in the baked-goods section of the store? That is a far cry from what *maman* probably did. She very likely walked to the local *boulangerie* where the smell of freshly-baked bread permeated the air and she no doubt emerged carrying a long, crusty loaf of French bread, unwrapped and in her hand.

Many institutions of learning consider the study of a nation's literature to be the single, ultimate goal toward which all language learning should be pointed. If by language we mean the method of communication of a people, then it is not its literature through which people communicate. The study of the history of languages, living and dead, reveals that no language has ever been able to survive unless it is rooted in the speech of the common man. His speech has more effect on keeping his language alive than does that of the poet who writes exquisite, beautifully constructed poems.

If language is not what is written, is not grammar, is not translation, and is not literature, what is it?

We know that language is a form and means of communication. It is intimately related to human beings since it is the universal and exclusive characteristic of man alone. It is the product of the human mind and the vocal apparatus which the human being possesses. It is the most important tool he has ever devised. It is the tool which enables him to make his living, build his home, and fashion his life. It is the instrument which gives order and organization to his thinking.

Charlton Laird tells us:

> . . . . the words being available, we learn to think with them, and rely upon them so much for practical purposes most people think only about things for which they have words and can think only in the directions for which they have words.

Each language, however, develops characteristics which are influenced by the cultural climate in which it is rooted. Children born in French-speaking families speak French, order their thinking and organize their lives in that language, and their brains think with words in that language with all their inherent nuances, overtones, and special connotations. Therefore, language belongs to the group at the same time it belongs to the individual. The language activity of the individual is dominated and proscribed by the language activity of the group to which he belongs. Its language becomes his language.

To come to a basic consideration of what we have just discussed, we can arrive at a definition of what language is; a definition which combines all the essentials.

Language is a *system* of human, vocal *behavior, culturally acquired* for the purposes of *transmitting information.* It is the universal, exclusive mark of man.

IMPLICATIONS

What are the pedagogical implications in this definition? Taking this statement and examining its parts will help to determine what it is necessary for the teacher to know about the processes involved in language.

Behavior, any kind of behavior, implies some knowledge of psychology. The foreign language teacher should be specifically concerned with the psychology of learning as it applies to vocal behavior. If language is a system the teacher must know something about linguistics in order to understand the key to the system or the underlying principles of the specific language being taught. If language is culturally acquired then the teacher will have to know something about the cultural anthropology, or the civilization in which the language under study has its roots and from which it grows. If language is to transmit information, the teacher will have to be concerned with concepts since it is through concepts that information is transmitted.

These, then, are the guidelines. Foreign language instruction must be aimed at engendering in the student those linguistic actions and reactions which give him the ability to receive and send culturally accurate information. The methods and materials which the teacher uses must be so designed as to help him in this many-sided task.

It is obvious that language teaching is largely concerned with the spoken word and with producing good speech behavior. Before the student can produce new and strange sounds he must hear them produced by someone else. He must hear good models often and he must be taught to discriminate among the sounds he hears. He must be taught to discern the subtleties and nuances of the sonority he hears before he can be expected to attempt to reproduce with any degree of accuracy the vibrations necessary for achieving the same results himself.

Good speech production depends upon the utilization of vocal muscles and the skills and habits which have been acquired through their proper use. Just as a student of the piano must develop muscles, skills, and habits to achieve competence, the language student, too, must develop skill through muscular control and habit formation. Habits are developed through innumerable repetitions, so many repetitions in fact that automaticity takes over and muscles perform without the mental activity which was necessary before the act became habit. The new materials of instruction must be organized to give proper emphasis and consideration to language as speech. Reading and writing should be introduced and developed at the right time and in relationship to the audio and lingual aspects of the foreign language.

As we have discovered, language is not just the noise we make with our vocal apparatus; this well-organized noise must render meaning between sender and receiver or there can be no communication. Americans and Englishmen both speak English yet they sometimes have difficulty understanding each other. For instance, when the Englishman says 1—no tipping, 2—subway, and 3—zebra, he really means 1—do not dump garbage here, 2—underpass, and 3—safe crossing for pedestrians. Obviously a foundation of common concepts is necessary for real understanding.

Concepts result from experiences, from the involvement of as many senses as possible i.e., the senses of sound, sight, smell, touch, and taste. Of course, the ideal way to have such experiences with a foreign language is to travel in the land where it is spoken and to live among the people. Since this is not feasible for the vast majority of students, provision for vicarious experiences must be made in the materials through which the student is to be instructed. These should give him as many cultural perceptions as possible to help him build concepts about the people and the land whose language he is learning. These materials must bring him as close to the real situation as possible (see Chapter 8).

As the accumulation of authentic observations becomes larger, the understanding of the language as well as the culture and civilization from which it grows becomes better. It is through this process that the instrument for communication is formed, strengthened, and augmented.

PRINCIPLES FOR TEACHING AND LEARNING A SECOND LANGUAGE

The foreign language teacher is more than just a teacher of language. He is a teacher of a second language to a monolingual student. He must understand not only the nature of language and its pedagogical implications, but he must also be cognizant of the special areas of emphasis which are inherent and unique to second-language instruction. Being aware of the following signposts is the first step toward establishing a sound foundation of methodological procedures.

Teaching does not necessarily result in learning. The teacher must recognize the difference between teaching and learning. This is particularly significant in foreign language pedagogy. For the first few years of language study most of what the student needs to learn must be taught to him in the classroom. He is entirely dependent on the teacher's guidance, instruction, and judgment. There is rarely an authoritative source outside of the language classroom to which he can turn for the information he seeks. He cannot learn new sounds, correct intonation, cadence, or any of the other paralinguistic phenomena so pertinent to language study by consulting the dictionary or the textbook. There is rarely anyone at home who is qualified to help him practice the sound which he has been taught in class. Even where the student is given practice records to use at home, he must be taught in class that which he is to practice at home. Furthermore, he cannot be sure he has practiced correctly until he comes back to class where his performance is appraised by the teacher.

The teacher of a second language must recognize that the teaching will not necessarily result in learning on the part of the student. The techniques for presenting information are not sufficient to inspire learning. The teacher will need to use various additional techniques and procedures which will help the student to learn, and to acquire what he is being taught.

In addition to acquiring techniques for stimulating and guiding the student to learn, the teacher must develop the insight to judge whether learning is taking place. The ability of the teacher to distinguish between his own performance and the performance by the student with the material he is being taught is without a doubt the single, most important quality a teacher of a second language can possess. He must gain the sensitivity to perceive whether the lesson is reaching the student, how much has reached him, and how much needs to be retaught. This crucial teaching skill can be acquired only through experience in the classroom, intelligent discernment, wisdom, and constant measurement.

Knowing about a foreign language does not necessarily result in the ability to use it: The second-language teacher must also be aware of the difference between knowing about a language and participating in it. Psychologists tell us that we can only learn to do by doing. One can develop the ability to speak a foreign language only by using it. Such competency cannot be achieved by learning rules of grammar, usually expressed in English, nor by giving reasons for the use of the various parts of speech, which is generally also in English.

The faculty for reading a foreign language is achieved only by reading in the foreign language. It can never be achieved by translation from the foreign language into the native language or vice versa. We learn what we practice. Active participation in each of the language skills—listening, speaking, reading and writing—is the only way to develop facility in each one.

The ability to understand language when it is spoken does not necessarily result in the ability to speak: The teacher of a second language must realize that hearing and speaking are two different skills and must be developed separately. The oral ability of the student cannot be developed by being exposed to more listening. Each of these skills involves different sections of the brain and depends on different sets of muscles, nerves, and organs. Hearing is passive, speaking is active. The skill of speaking takes longer to develop and is the first to deteriorate with disuse. A student may learn to understand without developing the ability to respond in the foreign language.

It is also important for the teacher of a second language to be cognizant of the fact that although the skills of hearing and speaking must be developed independently they are intricately related. The tongue cannot imitate what the ear does not hear but must practice what the ear does hear. Furthermore, it is not likely that the tongue will be able to imitate with exactness what the ear hears the first time. The ear will probably have to hear several times before the tongue will be able to imitate perfectly or nearly perfectly.

The ability to respond in a foreign language does not necessarily indicate comprehension: Understanding is the key stone of all foreign language study. The teacher must be on the alert constantly and unceasingly for proof of comprehension in everything the student hears, says, reads, or writes. The correctly-worded response in a foreign language classroom does not always indicate comprehension of the content of the material. Many teachers are prone to accept the answer which has perfect grammatical form as a sign of understanding of both the question and the answer.

Students can become very adept at constructing correct answers based on the question without grasping the thoughts involved. The teacher must recognize the danger of accepting these as the only proof of comprehension.

Frequent reference will be made, in the ensuing chapters, to what has been discussed above. Now that the principles for effective teaching and learning have been noted, we are ready to consider the aims and goals of foreign language teaching today.

SUGGESTED READINGS:

Brooks, Nelson, *Language and Language Learning* (New York, Harcourt, Brace & World, 1961).

Laird, Charlton, *The Miracle of Language* (New York, Fawcett World Library, 1960).

Modern Language Association, "Conference on Linguistics and Language Learning," May, 1963.

Nunnally, Jum C., *et al.*, "Psychological Implications of Word Usage," *Science*, Vol. 140 (May 17, 1963), 775–781.

For information on the 2,000 unwritten languages write to: The Wycliffe Bible Translators Linguistic Institute, Santa Ana, Calif.

3

THE APPROACH— LEARNING FOR PERFORMANCE

- The aims and goals of foreign language instruction are influenced by the nature and needs of society and not by educators.
- The teacher's role and responsibilities have changed in light of the new objectives.
- The learner must be made aware of his responsibilities.
- The new emphasis in foreign language instruction is teaching and learning for performance.
- The units of instruction must involve the instructor and learner in helping the latter acquire the skills necessary for performance.

The nature and needs of a society determine the goals toward which its educational system is directed. A course of study will be permitted to survive only if it is viable in the eyes of the public which is paying for it. The amount of money which is allocated for education by any community is a constant reminder of this fact. Therefore, it is actually the taxpayers who dictate educational policy in the light of the requirements and the current problems of the community. It then becomes the responsibility of the educator to carry out these policies and provide the kind of instruction which will bring about the results the public desires.

The need for communication in today's world spells out the goals toward which foreign language instruction in our country must be pointed. These aims are not the figment of the fertile imagination of some impractical educators who are ensconsed in ivory towers. These objectives are the results of very serious considerations of hard-headed, down-to-earth leaders engaged in solving some of our nation's problems.

It became obvious during World War II that language instruction, as it had been given up to that time, had not produced the foreign language-speaking personnel which the government needed. The U.S. Army had to set up crash programs to meet the emergency and thereupon two facts became apparent which were to shape the foreign language instruction of the future.

In the first place, people became aware of the fact that foreign languages were important to the national welfare. In the second place, the success of the methods used in the crash programs of the Army contrasted tellingly with the failure of the old-fashioned methods which had become entrenched in our schools.

The populace was beginning to evince the first glimmers of concern about foreign languages but the academic world was dragging its feet and, in some cases, was even moving backward. Despite the publicity given the "Army Method" during the war which aroused the public's interest in the study of other languages, in the six post-war years from 1947 to 1953, 46 institutions of higher learning dropped the language requirement for the Bachelor of Arts degree.

A small number of concerned, responsible citizens began to study the question and inquire into the causes of the inadequacies in foreign language instruction. They expressed anxiety over the situation in which the United States found itself because of the lack of personnel with competency in speaking foreign languages. In her speeches, Mrs. Franklin D. Roosevelt frequently stressed the necessity to learn to speak foreign languages. The General Federation of Women's Clubs called attention to the same need.

Discussions were held, and papers were written. The U.S. National Commission for UNESCO requested Professor William R. Parker to examine the foreign language situation in the United States and to write a work paper on the subject. The first edition of *The National Interest and Foreign Languages* was published in April, 1954. The essence of the problem was: *we need to understand people of other lands and we cannot understand them unless we learn to speak their language. Language instruction in the United States does not produce students with a knowledge and understanding of other people's mother tongues and their ways of life.*

In 1952, foreign language instruction received the first signs of official encouragement. In that year U.S. Commissioner of Education, Earl J. McGrath, admitted that he was wrong not to consider the study of foreign languages a very important element in general education. In that year, too, a Rockefeller grant was made to the Modern Language Association to help it begin an inquiry into the role which foreign languages could play in American life.

These issues did not get wide publicity and only minor changes were made in the national picture of foreign language instruction until 1957. It was at this time that Russia fired its memorable Sputnik and with it unwittingly launched our people into action. Foreign language instruction, along with mathematics, science, and guidance, was thrust into the uncomfortable limelight. Congress, aroused and concerned, moved to upgrade instruction in these areas. Educators in these subjects were called upon to cooperate in order to meet the needs of the nation. This situation was considered so grave that an act was passed with the words "defense" and "national" included in the title.

On September 2, 1958, the National Defense Act was passed which provided an initial $30 million in funds to strengthen, improve, and update instruction in foreign languages on all levels of education. The government of the United States was willing to spend that sum of money to get from the nation's foreign language instruction the kind of education it required to carry out its functions. The needs were clearly stated. More Americans with a real mastery of the foreign language skills are necessary so that our government can maintain contacts with the nations of the world and meet its international responsibilities.

The one word in this statement which requires examination is *skills*. The acquisition of skills is essential to meet the aims and goals for foreign language teaching. Which skills must the student master? Which skills will the teacher concentrate on strengthening?

EXAMINATION OF THE GOALS OF LANGUAGE TEACHING

Never before has man had such amazing instruments through which he can hear language and with which he can exchange ideas, such as the telephone, the radio, the television, the magnetic tape, and the film. Communication by sound is certainly one of the outstanding scientific achievements of our time. Distances and time are conquered with the use of such instantaneous exchange media as the space satellite, the micro-wave relay, and the overseas telephone. Obviously, in a world where man can and does communicate with all parts of the world by sound, the ability *to understand* a language when it is spoken is one of the basic skills which must be developed in every foreign language student.

Learning to express oneself verbally is most important in the study of a foreign language. This applies not only to the ability to formulate questions and answers in the foreign language, but also to the ability to express one's point of view, to defend one's opinions, and to take part in discussions and conversations. He who is unable to engage in such language activities cannot say that he knows a foreign language. Communication needs a sender as well as a receiver. Developing such ability *to speak* is unquestionably a skill to be perfected in every student who is studying a foreign language.

Knowing a foreign language suggests the capacity to read with ease and comprehension directly from the page as it is written. Trade journals, specialized periodicals, newsletters, pamphlets, brochures, and treatises are published in increasing numbers and imported literally by the ton each year. Direct correspondence has always been important and becomes more important as contacts increase. The beginning language student will very soon be the reader of this written matter. He will want to be able to read it easily and unhesitatingly, fully confident that he understands what he is reading. The ability *to read with comprehension directly in the foreign language* must, therefore, be a basic aim of language teaching.

The competence to read with ease and understanding leads to the desire to read the literary products, past and present, in that language. Such reading habits and inquisitiveness about the foreign literature last a lifetime.

As our intercourse with other nations increases, the need for written correspondence grows. More letters, commercial and private, cross the oceans by boat and plane than ever before. To-day's student will be engaged in business and commerce tomorrow. Undoubtedly, letters and other commercial papers for overseas consumption will have to be written. Carrying on such written exchange necessitates an ability to express one's ideas clearly and with accuracy on a variety of matters. A comparatively small number of our students will need to be able to write essays or dissertations in the foreign language but many of them will need to know how to write letters or cables or telegrams concerning everyday affairs. To *write accurately and correctly* is without a doubt a skill which must be developed in every student of foreign languages.

To understand the other man one needs to understand his way of life. One needs to know where he lives, how he lives, and how he maintains his life. Since the student's life is organized and limited by the language which he and his countrymen speak (see page 22), another goal of language teaching must be to *develop* through the foreign language, *an appreciation* of *the culture and civilization* of the people whose language he is learning. Without this his knowledge of the language, no matter how letter perfect it is, may be based on false premises and built on inaccurate conceptions (see page 10).

THE TEACHER'S ROLE AND RESPONSIBILITIES

In the light of the new objectives of foreign language instruction the teacher's role and responsibilities have taken on new and different dimensions. The teacher is responsible for seeing that the student acquires all the language skills which have been discussed above: *comprehension of the spoken word, speaking, reading, and writing.* Certainly at the initial stages of instruction and even beyond that, he is the sole source of knowledge. The student can only be expected to give back what the teacher has given him (see page 14).

To learn to speak a foreign language is a skill which takes more time to develop than any of the other language skills. Another skill, closely related and almost as difficult, is learning to comprehend a foreign language as it is being spoken. It is obvious, then, that the teacher and the student must devote more time to these two areas than to the other phases of language education. These activities must engage the student's time from the very beginning of his study of the language. He must continue to perfect and maintain his control of these skills throughout his entire course.

Language skills are developed just as any other skill is developed—by guidance, practice, correction, more guidance, more practice, and more correction, over and over again until perfection or control is achieved. One learns to play a musical instrument or work a machine or manipulate a tool by the same process.

Because the learner has no one else but the teacher to turn to, the instructor's responsibilities to the student are manifold. First, the teacher must present the language so that it is meaningful to the student. The teacher must know and make use of those devices which will infuse meaning into the sounds he is presenting (see page 39). Language must be presented to the student in a manner which will enable him to imitate what he hears. To do this well, the teacher must have accurate control of the sound and linguistic systems of the language. He must also be familiar with those pedagogical procedures which give him insight into how to organize and to delimit those segments of language which he will require the student to imitate and learn to manage (see page 42).

One can only learn to understand spoken language by hearing it. And one can only learn to speak a language by imitating those who speak it. To achieve control over comprehension of the spoken word and speaking within the limited amount of time which the student and the instructor have together, the teacher must use the foreign language exclusively and require the same of the student during class time. This will give the student as much contact time with the language as possible. Every word which is not spoken in the foreign language by teacher or student decreases the time available for hearing and imitating it.

Secondly, the teacher must guide the student in his practice, judge his performance, correct his errors, and guide him to more practice. To do this he must be secure in his own knowledge of the phonology and the grammatical structures of the language. He must also perceive the pupil's difficulties and be capable of selecting appropriate procedures for correcting them. Mere practice and repetition can deteriorate into meaningless, boring activity. Guiding the student to observe generalities from the language he is practicing is one of the most important responsibilities of the foreign language teacher (see page 66). Teaching the student to become aware of what he hears and imitates and to make deductions is the keystone upon which language education is built. Such training should begin on the first day of instruction and continue through all phases of it.

Thirdly, since classroom drill and practice is essential to the learning process, the teacher must see that each student gets sufficient opportunity to participate in this kind of activity. To do this effectively, without producing boredom and apathy, the teacher must have knowledge of a variety of procedures and devices so that the practice continues until control is achieved without bringing the class to the point of unproductive fatigue (see page 45).

The teacher must also establish a set of hand and arm signals or gestures which are understood by everyone. Certain hand motions should elicit responses from the whole class, others from half the class, still others from certain rows or from individuals. These gestures do for the teacher what similar motions do for the conductor of a chorus. They bring about the kind of activity that the teacher requires. They activate the performance of the whole class or parts of it. They maintain the desired tempo. The proper communication by hand signals between teacher and students makes for a smooth, lively, and well-paced lesson.

Fourthly, to help the student develop the ability to understand the written language directly from the printed page, it is imperative that the teacher know and use devices which never take the student out of the framework of the foreign language (see Chapter 7). He must not resort to translation in lieu of reading and writing activities. To acquaint the student with commercial as well as literary language, the teacher must be knowledgeable about the newspapers and periodicals which are produced abroad. Selections from these should be used as reading materials for class and homework.

The skill of writing should be developed by using topics of everyday interest as well as literary subjects. In this area the teacher must develop techniques which so guide the student that he never has to leave the foreign language to develop his theme or express his ideas (see pages 113–123).

The greatest responsibility any teacher has to any student is to inspire him to put forth his best effort to learn. Few students will make greater demands on themselves than those that the teacher makes on them. They will only give back what they have discerned the teacher considers essential. This is particularly true of the language student because he is so dependent on the teacher's conduct and judgment.

Does the teacher set great store by memorization by rote? The student will oblige by memorizing by rote.

Does the teacher put a premium on grammar facts rather than on fluency? The student will concentrate his efforts to learn the former rather than to develop the latter.

Does the teacher use English because he thinks it is faster to explain in English and easier to understand? Then that is what the student will do, too. And why not, if it is faster and easier for the teacher, it is faster and easier for him, too?

Does the teacher reward and praise enthusiasm, ingenuity, good deductions, and analogies? This will be reflected in the student's effort and performance.

He will endeavor to please the teacher by imitating him and giving him what he thinks he wants.

THE LEARNER'S ROLE AND RESPONSIBILITIES

The change in emphasis in foreign language instruction affects the role and responsibility of the learner, too. What he can expect to learn, how he is to perform, and what is required of him in class and at home must be made clear to him before he embarks on this study (see page 35).

We are told that learning is the process whereby habits are formed and knowledge is acquired. Since language learning is largely habit formation which must be acquired in the classroom, the student's role revolves around active participation in those experiences which are repeated and practiced there.

Students are educated by their own physical and mental activities. The teacher is responsible for stimulating those actions by providing the proper situations and conditions for learning. The student, however, must be made aware of the fact that he alone is responsible for applying himself to the learning situation.

In the initial stages he is answerable for listening attentively, and for recognizing and responding to the teacher's signals and gestures. His activities will include imitating, repeating, practicing, and memorizing. He will participate and perform and derive as much benefit as possible from the activity in the classroom.

Very early in his experience in the acquisition of language habits he will begin to understand the learning process by observing and by trying to make deductions from the language he is repeating and manipulating. "Finding out for oneself" is a basic tenet of learning. Experimentation shows that the number of repetitions necessary to fix desired responses depends on the attitudes of the learner. Experience shows that students like drills that are interesting and purposeful. Repetition takes on a new measure of importance when the student knows that through this exercise he is expected to find something out for himself. He will learn to observe so that he can formulate generalizations which will become a basis for more learning and which will effect control over what he has already learned.

He will gain deeper understanding of the language he has

acquired by engaging in manipulative drills. Through these he will learn how to handle the structures of the language. Repetitive and manipulative drills should facilitate recall of what has been learned and develop automaticity of response.

The ability to apply what he has learned to control is proof that the student has learned. When he can transfer what he has learned to similar situations, when he can communicate his own ideas by using freely and spontaneously the structures he has repeated and manipulated in drills and exercises, he shows that he has acquired command over the language he has been taught. For instance, if, after studying a unit on the family he can engage in free conversation about his own family, he demonstrates that he has learned and can control that segment of language.

THE PERFORMANCE APPROACH

We who are language specialists and pride ourselves on knowing how to use words have unfortunately acquired a professional vocabulary which engenders misunderstanding among ourselves as well as with the public. We use words which do not convey our thoughts. Some of us use the word "method" when we mean materials, and some of us use the word "approach" when we mean methods and techniques. We were most naïve when we accepted names like "audio-lingual " and "aural-oral" to describe the philosophical basis upon which *all* our teaching procedures are built.

We need to define our terms specifically and clearly. We need to re-examine our professional glossary. We must be careful to choose the proper words for our ideas, if we hope to understand and be understood.

It is important to distinguish among the three most often confused terms: the audio-lingual method, MLA, and A-LM. Unfortunately, the similarity of the initial letters in all these names has led to much confusion.

The term "audio-lingual method" refers to techniques and practices which a teacher uses in the classroom to develop in his students the abilities to speak and comprehend the spoken word. It does not refer to any particular course of materials. A teacher can use audio-lingual techniques with very traditional materials (see Appendix A).

MLA refers to the Modern Language Association which is a learned society in the field of the Humanities. It exists for the purpose of advancing literary and linguistic studies in English and Foreign Languages. MLA publishes scholarly books and produces reports, manuals, films, and other materials dealing with the teaching of language and linguistics.

A-LM refers to a course published by a commercial publishing house which uses those letters as a trademark. This publisher is not associated with MLA. Although the course incorporates audio-lingual techniques, it is only one among many new courses of materials on the market and is not to be equated with the audio-lingual method. Criticism of A-LM or any other new program should not be considered a condemnation of the audio-lingual method.

Much has been written since 1958 about the New Approach. It implies a new direction in which we are moving to arrive at our new goals. The names "audio-lingual" and "aural-oral" apply to procedures or materials and they deal with only half of our story. They describe only two of the four skills with which we are involved. These terms do not include, even by implication, a most important organ through which learning normally takes place, the eye.

All our teaching is headed toward developing in our students the ability to perform. Performance in all aspects of the language skills is the objective of the new approach, and the direction in which we are going. An appropriate appellation, I suggest, would be **the performance approach.**

The methods which we use to inspire performance must be as varied, subtle, and as many-faceted as are our aims. Methods are the procedures, the techniques through which the teacher instructs, and are not to be confused with materials. The same materials can be handled in as many ways as there are teachers using them. Each teacher brings to the instructional process his attitudes and competencies which are the result of his own experiences with people and society.

Good teaching is not a mechanical process. It involves a

teacher operating in the complex interpersonal relationships of the classroom. Satisfactory methods depend, to a great extent, upon how the teacher comprehends the nature and conditions of learning coupled with his instructional aims and purposes. The skillful and sensitive teacher will set the stage for desirable, appropriate, and satisfactory learning experiences. Always keeping his eye on the goals, he directs, coaches, and rehearses until the student performs smoothly. He may even have to reset the entire stage and bring on a whole new bag of tricks if he sees that learning is not taking place against the old stage set.

The student brings to the learning process many attitudes, biases, and concepts based on his own experiences. No one method will reach them all. The artful teacher will use many methods, and will show many sides of the material he is teaching so as to reach the interest of as many learners as possible. The success or failure of his procedures will be seen in the light of the effects on the learner, and in the changes in his performance. If he has learned, he will perform well; if he has not been reached, he will perform imperfectly or not at all. This may be as much a reflection on the teacher and his procedures and techniques as it is a reflection on the student and his ability to learn and perform.

LIFE SITUATIONS AS UNITS OF INSTRUCTION

Since language is related to life and is used in life situations, it is reasonable to assume that we will have to relate our teaching to life situations in order to make our instruction meaningful and purposeful to the student. The ability to control the kind of situation which confronts or will confront an individual in actual life must be the central theme of our units of work. We are not concerned with developing habits, skills, knowledge, attitudes, and interests in a vacuum. Learning must be directed toward developing all these abilities in order to be able to perform in real life situations and to effect desirable responses to them.

It is of the utmost importance that the student recognize the need for that which is to be learned. If he feels that the theme is real and significant he will respond with significant, purposeful activity.

Dealing with a life situation unit of work makes the difference between teaching sets of unrelated activities and providing an experience which unifies, coordinates, and controls these activities for the purpose of attaining a specific objective. Learning the future tense of verbs cannot become significant until these verbs are seen by the student in a situation where he is desirous of telling about an incident which is to take place sometime in the future.

The unit which simulates real situations helps the teacher place the emphasis of usage on those language activities which will be coordinated and correlated to cope with the situation. It focuses learning upon the student's needs. The student learns to perform by performing and not by talking about form and structure. It makes possible a variety of learning activities.

Instruction by units minimizes piecemeal teaching. It puts the emphasis on unity of material related to a central idea or concept and not on a series of disconnected grammatical subjects which are unnatural, contrived, and not easily put to use. Individual lessons are not taught in isolation but as they relate and contribute to the understanding of the central theme.

Teaching through situational units requires two kinds of parallel lesson plans. One plan outlines the entire, overall unit in broad terms and delineates the purposes, objectives, materials, and projects of the entire topic. The other plans are the detailed, day-by-day lessons which indicate specific methodology, structures, and drills which must be covered in order to achieve the purposes and objectives outlined in the plan of the unit.

Teaching by life situations should help the teacher break away from the domination of one textbook or one set of materials. It calls for a range of materials which can provide cohesion and wholeness whether they are found in pictures, records, newspapers, magazines, or in other such sources.

It is one thing to talk about aims and goals, about teacher's and student's responsibilities, and about the philosophical foundation of language teaching. It is another thing to practice what we preach.

The teaching process is complex and complicated, and through the welter of procedures, techniques, and details we are apt to lose sight of what we are trying to accomplish. "Keep your eye on the ball, but never lose sight of the goal," is what the coach tells the team. This is what we must tell ourselves. Every activity we ask our students to engage in should be meaningful and purposeful in the light of our objectives. The student must perform to gain control of all the language skills in the language he is learning. Anything else we ask of him is of little value.

SUGGESTED READINGS:

Guidelines to Regulations (Revised 1963), National Defense Education Act of 1958, Title III. Sections 301–304.

Jones, Arthur J., *et al.*, *Principles of Unit Construction* (New York, Mc-Graw-Hill, 1939).

Lee, Florence Henry (ed.), *Principles and Practices of Teaching in Secondary Schools* (Philadelphia, McKay, 1964).

"Modern Foreign Languages in the Comprehensive Secondary School," National Association of Secondary School Principals Committee on Curriculum Planning and Development, NASSP-NEA, Washington, D.C.

Parker, William Riley, *The National Interest and Foreign Languages*, Department of State Publication 7324 (U.S. Government Printing Office, Washington, D.C., 1962).

4
THE PRE-READING
PERIOD

- A pre-reading period of instruction is necessary for developing in the student the skills of comprehension and speaking.
- An orientation to this pre-textbook period is important for the parents and the community as well as for the student.
- The homework assignments during this period can be very valuable even if they do not require work in the foreign language.
- There are many factors which determine the length of the pre-reading period.
- The teacher must plan methods and materials for this period so that performance by the student in comprehending and speaking will result.

THE RATIONALE

The two skills which take the longest time to develop are: the ability *to understand* a foreign language when it is spoken by natives at their normal speed; and the ability *to speak* a foreign language so that it can be understood by natives as well as by others who speak the language. These two competencies are the foundation upon which all the other skills are built. It is therefore essential that every language student be given the fullest opportunity to develop them.

The pre-reading period of instruction gives the student and the teacher the time necessary for concentrating on the practice of the sound skills of the language. Only after the student has these under control is he ready to go on to the other phases of his language study.

During this period the student should be engaged in listening activities which enable him to recognize the foreign sounds. He would thus be taught to discriminate between the foreign sounds and would learn to discern the difference between them and their nearest English equivalent.* During this time the student should also be involved in imitating the foreign language as he hears it spoken by a model. His entire attention should be devoted to perfecting his knowledge of the sound system of the foreign language. This includes pronunciation, intonation, rhythm, and cadence of the language. He would learn, too, something about the hand gestures and body motions which are peculiar, pertinent, and important to that spoken language.

The best place to acquire this knowledge would be, of course, in the land where the language is spoken. There the student would be surrounded by native speakers and completely cut off from his native tongue. He would be thoroughly immersed in the foreign language. Since this is impossible for most of our students, we can do the next best thing, which is to create an island of foreign language in our classroom. Here we should attempt to simulate the foreign atmosphere as much as possible in order to shield the student from the interference of his own native language.

Our students come to us with very fixed language habits. They have acquired the structure and sound system of their own language. They have learned how these sounds relate to a set of written symbols. These symbols have become so interrelated in the student's mind with the sounds they represent that they are not recognized as symbols but as sounds. If we are to be successful in teaching our student another sound system, we must divorce him, while in the foreign language classroom, from the symbols he has learned. The symbols he verbalizes are the sound values of his native language. He must be free of everything that relates to the sound of his mother tongue.

It is for this reason that the student should be given a pre-reading period of instruction where he does not see any written

---

* In this instance the use of English in the classroom is necessary for establishing pairs of words which point up differences in pronunciation between English and the foreign language.

word. At this point, since he has not yet acquired a sure command of the sound system of the foreign language, the written word would only elicit sounds which relate to his native language and not to the foreign language. This is the kind of interference we are trying to avoid. By imitating and practicing sounds without seeing any written symbols the student would not be tempted to transfer the sound values from the one system to the other.

A pre-reading period will strengthen the student's reading ability when he gets to see the printed page. Reading specialists tell us that we need to hear sub-vocally the pronunciation of the words we are reading in order to get comprehension from the printed page. As Edgar Dale tells us in his *News Letter,* "you must have a word in your ear before you can have that word in your eye." Where the command of actual speech is imperfect, reading is delayed and understanding is faulty. As our eye scans the printed phrases we subliminally form the sounds and hear them in our inner consciousness. When our eyes encounter words which are unfamiliar to our tongue and ear we are stopped in our tracks. We hesitate in our reading as we try to pronounce the word, hoping that the sound will bring recognition of the word and its meaning. We puzzle over it for a while. In the meantime, we have lost our train of thought and very likely we have to go back to the beginning of the sentence and start all over again. If we hope to be able to read directly from the printed page, smoothly, easily, and with comprehension, it is very important that we first learn the sound system of the language.

Some teachers neglect to devote enough time to an intensive pre-reading period in the mistaken belief that the sight of the written word helps the student to remember the foreign language better. New material is thus presented orally and graphically at the same time and the student hears the sounds in the new lesson as he simultaneously sees their written forms.

For all of the reasons already given, such practice will tend to hinder rather than help the student master the oral aspect of the language he is studying. Furthermore, in this procedure the importance of achieving good pronunciation is minimized and often neglected while the act of reading is emphasized.

Leonard Bloomfield in *Language* tells us that if one tries to learn to read and speak at the same time, one's progress toward both skills is likely to be delayed.

The ability to speak affects one's ability to write. One cannot write unless the sounds of the words in their relationship to one another reverberate somewhere in the back of one's head. Very few people can write even in their own language without "mulling it over." In a foreign language it is most important that the student have a command of the spoken word if he hopes to arrange and rearrange his thoughts several times before putting pen to paper. The arranging and rearranging is a silent verbalization which must take place before anything meaningful can be written.

INTRODUCTORY ORIENTATION

For all of the reasons indicated above, the student should be started in the study of the foreign language without resorting to a book. Since he does not yet know the written form of the language he should not be required to write in class, nor should he be required to do any written homework in the foreign language. This is radically different from the manner in which he is expected to conduct himself in other classes where he is given a textbook the first day of the term, where he takes written notes in class on which he will be tested, and where he is given assignments to be written at home.

So that he can understand what we are doing and so that he can know what is expected of him in this new, strange learning situation, the student should be given an introductory orientation before he actually begins the study of the language. If he knows why we are keeping him from seeing the printed word for a period of time he will not constantly "nag" for a book. If he understands that he is not expected to know how to write at this time and that he will not be tested on it, he will not secretly devise his own phonetic system for taking notes. If he knows what we are attempting to achieve he will not carry a distorted message back home to his friends and his family.

It is equally important to orient the parents to the performance approach as well as to the pre-reading period of language instruction. Parents who themselves have never had any contact with the new methods may misinterpret our classroom activities. Students reflect the attitudes of their parents, their older sisters and brothers. The criticism expressed in the family circle and among friends colors the student's attitude toward the teacher and the material being used for teaching. A meeting with parents in which the objectives are clearly stated and in which methods and procedures are explained and even demonstrated will help the parent and student to understand the aims of foreign language instruction. A good rapport can thus be established between teacher and student and teacher and parent.

THE HOMEWORK QUESTION
IN THE NON-READING PERIOD

The importance which a student and his parent place upon a course is often illogically measured by the amount of homework that is assigned each night. The prestige of a major subject is unfortunately diminished if there is little or no homework assigned. Moreover, if the student is given no homework during the pre-reading period he may adopt the attitude that assignments in the foreign language class are not important and he may neglect to do his homework after the pre-reading period is over.

These, however, are not the only reasons for assigning homework during the pre-reading period. Since during this period the student should not be expected to do homework in the foreign language, this can be an ideal time to engage him in activities which can be done in English. These assignments can help to build up his knowledge of the culture of the people whose language he is studying and their way of life. He may be required to read books on the geography or history of the foreign country. This can also be a good time to learn something about its great men, musicians, artists, painters, etc.

Outline maps in which he locates cities, rivers, mountains, etc., can teach him much about the topography of the land he is studying. Research projects on national holidays, regions, industries, and exports and imports are interesting and profitable topics for students to explore. Other good and important projects could concern various aspects of the government, heads of state, departments, etc. The film stars and popular singers, dancers, and other figures in the entertainment world are always of great interest to the student. Assignments of this kind are not "make work" for the student. They can contribute greatly to his understanding of the culture and the civilization from which the language he is studying has come.

THE LENGTH OF THE PRE-READING PERIOD

How long should the pre-reading period last? How long should the student be kept from seeing the written word? How long should the teacher engage the student in purely audio and oral activities? No specific time limit can be recommended to suit every situation. It will vary from teacher to teacher, from class to class, and from school to school. The length of the pre-reading period depends on the following important factors.

One determining factor can be the *age of the student*. The young student who has not yet developed very firm habits of learning from the written page can be given a longer pre-reading period than the adult who has studied everything all his life by seeing it first in written form. The high school student who has already acquired more fixed visual habits of study should be given a shorter period than the younger junior high school student whose habits of study are less fixed. The child in the fourth grade should be given the longest period of all.

Another determining factor can be the *complexity of the sound system* of the language under study. Where the sounds are very different from English it will take longer to master them and consequently the period prior to going to the printed page should be longer than it would be for a language whose sound system is not too different from that of English. In a language where the student can imitate the sounds with comparative ease because they are very similar to those in English, the pre-reading period can be fairly short.

Another factor which can determine the length of this period is the *aptitude and receptivity of the student*. The student who is quick to imitate correctly and reproduce the new sounds accurately and fluently, can be ready for reading sooner than the one who is slower to imitate without error.

Still another factor can be the *teacher's ability* to handle this period of instruction. The teacher who is new at conducting a purely "sound" phase of language instruction will no doubt have a shorter pre-reading period than a teacher who has had previous experience with it. As this teacher becomes more adept at handling the audio and oral procedures, the length of time devoted to this kind of teaching will probably increase.

The teacher's resources also play a part in determining the amount of time to be spent on these activities. If he is teaching from a traditional text and has to prepare his own supplementary audio materials, he is more apt to shorten the period than if he has materials prepared and ready to use.

The pre-reading period should be at least as long as it takes the student to gain control over the sound system of the language. It is inefficient to allow him to proceed to the reading and writing phases of language study until he can reproduce the sounds of the language with a considerable degree of fluency and accuracy.

No matter how long or short the pre-reading period is, it should be an integral part of the syllabus. The student should be made to feel that it is an important, intrinsic part of the course of study. It should be arranged so that it leads directly to the printed word.

Even after the student has been introduced to the written word he should continue to practice his audio and oral skills. In reality there should be a pre-reading phase before all reading and writing activities (see page 97). All reading material should be presented orally first, so that the student can comprehend and imitate before he sees the selection in written form.

ORGANIZATION OF METHODS AND MATERIALS FOR THE PRE-READING PERIOD

The emphasis during this period of instruction is on the spoken word and on performance in this area by the student. Since linguistics is the science which deals with phenomena of language, and psychology tells us much about learning behavior, these are the best sources for guidance to help us in organizing methods and procedures for effective language teaching. These procedures may be used by any teacher and are not intended to be used only with the newer courses of instruction. The methods described below can be used equally well by the teacher who is using the traditional textbook.

Presentation

What kind of material should the teacher select for use in oral practice and drill? Oral or conversational prose is very different from written prose. Spoken language is not on the same level as written language. When one writes one has had time to think through, polish, rewrite, and produce sentences which are perfectly formed, to the point where they no longer resemble normal speech. The author does not achieve such perfection when he expresses the same thoughts orally. The necessity for quick, spontaneous production does not give him the time to refine his oral language to the degree he did the written. His spoken language would, no doubt, contain shortened forms, less polished structures, and more junctures and linkings than the language which he wrote.

For this reason language which was not written to be spoken does not serve the teacher well for oral drill and practice. It does not provide the student with the phenomena which are natural and normal to spoken language. Conversations, dialogues, and plays are better suited for developing oral ability than are short stories, novels, or articles which were written to be read silently.

Since it is impossible to present by written symbols the true character of oral prose, the teacher has much to add to the selection he chooses. The written language cannot express intonation and stress and does not indicate phrasing, linking, slurring, and many other vocal subtleties. These the teacher must provide in his presentation. All new material should first be presented orally. This applies not only to material which is being taught to beginning students but also to that material which is being presented for the first time to intermediate and even advanced students.

The first presentation, although oral must also be meaningful. If the student is to become interested and enthusiastic, the language which he hears must have significance for him. Here the teacher can, without ever resorting to English, show his ingenuity by using whatever devices, gestures, pictures, and objects he deems necessary for bringing meaning to the sounds he is presenting to the student. The importance of presenting meaningful language to the class cannot be stressed too strongly. If the students do not appear to grasp meaning from the devices the teacher has chosen for the first presentation, some other scheme should be devised. A presentation scheme which does not convey meaning the first time will not become more meaningful if it is repeated exactly the same way several times.

For instance, suppose the teacher wants to show the class the meaning of the following sentence which appears in the selection to be studied: "The fishermen of Janitizio spread out their nets on poles to dry." The use of a good, large, clear picture of the island which shows the nets on the poles may not necessarily convey the complete meaning, i.e., that the fishermen stretch out the nets on the poles. The repetition of the sentence several times while holding up the same picture will not make the meaning any clearer to the student who did not grasp it the first time. The teacher must resort to other devices. For example, a gesture of the arms might clarify the word "spread out." The use of a window pole and a blackboard ruler together with the gesture could bring meaning to a larger segment of the sentence; that of spreading out the nets on the poles. Pointing to the fishermen in the picture may help the student identify the word as it is being pronounced. Several repetitions of the sentence with the use of such gestures and objects followed by a second showing of the picture will reach more students than did the first presentation of the picture alone. Sometimes a third, fourth, or more methods of presentation with different devices may be necessary before "the light dawns."

Dramatized, visualized presentations are interesting and give the teacher the chance to inject variety into the teaching process. Since much of our language instruction is routine drill and repetition, the presentation of new material can afford the occasion for humor or levity. It also gives the teacher the opportunity to bring all kinds of interesting materials into the classroom. The use of proper visuals is invaluable for helping the instructor teach culture with language (see pages 84–91).

The thing to remember is that a class is made up of individuals, each with his own background and frames of reference. One single kind of presentation may not reach all the students. If they do not grasp the meaning of the material which is being presented at this point, it is better to stay with it until they do than to proceed. The association of sound and meaning must be effected. The ingenious teacher will find many ways to evoke comprehension and the reward of such presentations are many. Teaching the student to listen and reach for meaning is good training (see pages 109–112). Presenting new material as many times and in as many ways as is necessary for almost the entire class to comprehend is time well spent. It will save many hours of reteaching later on.

Once the class appears to have grasped the meaning, the new material should be presented several more times from beginning to end, without interruptions, with or without illustrative devices. Only after he has heard new material from eight to ten times can the student be expected to reproduce it with any degree of accuracy.

Choral Mimicry

When the class has heard the new material several times it is ready to attempt imitating the teacher's model. The teacher should begin by pronouncing the first sentence of the selection clearly and at normal speed. He should indicate the rising or falling melody or intonation on the board. He can use patterns of dashes ($\_-$) or dots (. · ·) or arrows ($\nearrow\nearrow$) which indicate the rising or falling inflection as well as the stressed words in the sentence. The teacher should repeat the sentence several times, clearly and at normal speed, pointing to the diagram on the board to fix the melody and rhythm of the sentence in the ears of the students. After several repetitions, he should gesture by a prearranged, recognizable hand signal indicating that he wants the whole class to mimic him, imitating exactly the pronunciation, melody, rhythm, and speed.

He should repeat the sentence the same way as many as

eight times. After each repetition he signals the class to repeat after him. *They should not repeat with him but after him.* This enables the teacher to hear the class perform, something which he cannot do if he is talking at the same time that they are talking. It is good practice for the teacher to walk around the room as he is conducting this part of the presentation so that he can hear and be heard by the students who are seated at the sides and at the rear of the room.

He should stop the chorus to correct sounds, intonation, and rhythm. If the sentence proves to be too long for correct, smooth recall or repetition he should teach it phrase by phrase. In order to preserve the intonation, he should teach it by reverse build-up, beginning with the phrases at the end and working up to the beginning of the sentence.

For example, the sentence in French *"Je vais à la boulangerie pour acheter du pain"* would be divided and taught as follows:

The last phrase *du pain* would be taught and drilled first.

$$\dots du \; \overset{\searrow}{pain}.$$

The next to the last phrase *pour acheter* would be drilled next.

$$\dots pour \; \overset{\nearrow}{acheter} \; du \; \overset{\searrow}{pain}.$$

Then *à la boulangerie*

$$\dots \overset{\longrightarrow}{à \; la \; boulangerie} \; \overset{\longrightarrow}{pour \; acheter} \; du \; \overset{\searrow}{pain}.$$

And then the whole sentence.

$$\overset{\longrightarrow}{Je \; vais \; à \; la \; boulangerie} \; \overset{\longrightarrow}{pour \; acheter} \; du \; \overset{\searrow}{pain}.$$

After about eight repetitions the teacher can indicate by a recognizable hand signal that the class is to repeat the sentence without him.

With sufficient repetition, when the class seems to be able to perform smoothly as a group, the teacher should call for repetition by one half of the class while the other half listens. After several repetitions, the roles are reversed. From half chorus, the performance can proceed to rows. One row repeats, while the others listen; then the teacher engages the individual student. Each of these changes should be made smoothly, without loss of time or slackening of tempo by using a system of hand signals which has been carefully explained to the class. Double or triple repetitions may also be indicated by hand signals.

Each sentence of the selection should be taken consecutively and separately and treated as described above until all the sentences of the selection have been modeled and thoroughly imitated by the class. During all phases of choral repetition the teacher must be very sure to correct errors of pronunciation and intonation. The performance should be kept moving at normal speed and smoothly.

Choral imitation serves a very important purpose in language teaching and learning. The full chorus gives the student the chance to practice aloud in anonymity until he has taken hold of the sound and speed of the sentence. He is spared the embarrassment of a bad solo performance.

Choral repetition gives everyone the chance to perform. Every student has the opportunity to repeat many times. Every student gets the chance to hear the model and imitate immediately after hearing while it is still fresh in his ears.

By dint of the numerous repetitions which choral response makes possible, the students begin to sense the word order of the foreign language, the sentence structure, and the constructions of words and phrases. They learn to accept the language as it is. They begin to see that correct intonation, rhythm, and cadence are as important as pronunciation. They begin to realize the importance of mimicry in foreign language learning.

Questions and Answers

The science of linguistics tells us that language is a habit which is produced by appropriate reaction to external stimuli.

The student, if he is to acquire the habit, must have opportunities to respond correctly.

Speech is psychological. What comes out of the mouth and the manner and form in which it emerges is affected by what takes place in the brain. We know that we speak better when we are not tense and apprehensive. We also speak better when we know that our words are falling on receptive, friendly ears. We tighten up and develop "blocks" when we feel that our listener is looking for errors in what we are saying.

The empathy which is established between the teacher and the foreign language student is a very important factor in language learning and should never be lost sight of in their relationship. Putting the student at ease, giving him a feeling of helpful friendliness instead of unfriendly fault-finding lies behind the practice of supplying the student with the right answer in the early stages of his language training. He develops a confidence in himself, he performs without fear of criticism by the teacher or ridicule by his peers. Later on in his language study when he has gained confidence in his performance, he may be given more opportunity to attempt a trial-and-error method. This, however, is not recommended for the student at the beginning of his experience with a foreign language when he needs all the guidance and confidence he can get from his teacher.

Creating situations where he flounders and fumbles and in which he is penalized for producing incorrect responses is not conducive to establishing good language habits. We have said that speech is psychological behavior as well as muscular activity. Unsure, hesitant, and incorrect performance frustrates and discourages the student and develops in him an apathetic, if not antagonistic, attitude toward foreign language instruction. Correctness of performance and the satisfaction derived therefrom are the two ingredients necessary for promoting enthusiastic learning. In order to acquire good linguistic behavior the student should be in a situation where he can produce only correct responses and where he gets satisfaction from his performance.

After the student has mimicked the selection until he can reproduce the pronunciation, the intonation, rhythm, and cadence he will be ready for further manipulation of the language he has imitated. He is ready to use the language he has been repeating and mimicking. This will take the form of answering questions based on the selection he has been studying.

In the early stages of language instruction in order to avoid incorrect and fumbling responses the teacher will supply both the question and the answer. The student will learn both the question and the correct answer. This is good pedagogy for several reasons. It starts a good language habit by supplying the response immediately to the external stimulus (the question). With sufficient practice of both, the student should be able to supply the answer to that question almost automatically whenever he meets that stimulus.

Supplying the correct answer is an economical teaching procedure. Class time is used to the maximum advantage of all the students. Everyone learns more from practicing the correct answer than from waiting for a hesitating student to formulate an incorrect one. And experience shows that the teacher has to supply the correct answer in the long run anyhow.

The devices for teaching the questions and answers are the same as those for teaching the sentences of the selection. The class practices, repeats, and mimics the question and the answer first by full chorus, then by half chorus, then by row, and finally by individuals. (This practice is repeated for each set of questions and answers.) When everyone has had sufficient practice and the question and the answer can be spoken almost automatically, the procedure can be varied in several ways.

The Chain Drill

The teacher starts a chain drill by asking the question of one student. After that student has answered, the teacher asks that student to ask the question of another student. This process can be shortened by a hand signal which indicates that one student is to ask the question of another student. That student answers and turns to ask the question of another student and so on through several student question-and-answer responses.

After the chain has asked and answered the same question five or six times the procedure may be modified slightly for a change of pace. The question can be shortened to a more conversational form as follows:

> A student asks: At what time did you eat breakfast this morning?
> Answer: I ate breakfast at six, (turning to the next student) and you?

The question then becomes "and you" instead of "At what time did you eat breakfast this morning?" This chain drill can continue for a few more students. A chain drill is a good teaching device for introducing some variety. Here the student and not the teacher gets the opportunity to ask the question.

Chain drills can be used frequently but they should not be too long. Seven or eight student responses are usually enough. They should not be carried on always in the same order. They should not always start at the same point in the room and proceed in the same direction.

Please Ask Me That Question

This is a very useful sentence for the teacher whenever he wants to break into a chain drill for any reason. When the chain has gone to seven or eight students and the teacher wishes to end it he can ask (in the foreign language, of course) "please ask me that question" and when he answers the question, the chain can end there. Or the teacher can answer the question, and then address it to a student in another part of the room. This breaks up the predictable order of the chain and creates variety and a change of pace.

When the teacher sees that the pronunciation or intonation of the question or answer needs correction or reinforcement he can ask the student "please ask me that question." This gives him the opportunity to again model the response. He can thus call attention to those aspects which need correction and drill them. When he thinks that he has made his points clear he can start the chain going again by directing the question to another student.

The teacher may want to show the class how to add to the answer which has gone to several students already. This may be done as follows:

Q (by student): Is your mother home?

A (by another student): No, she is not home.

Teacher: Please ask me that question. (to student who has just answered)

Q: Is your mother home?

A (by teacher): No, she is not home, she went to the store.

This longer answer will then be practiced several times before the chain is started again.

The please-ask-me-that-question technique can be used by the ingenious teacher for many purposes: to correct, to show the student new answers, to combine several shorter sentences into one long response, to vary the order of the chain drill, and to show the student how to make use of previously learned material.

Directing the Questions and Answers

Directing the student by suggesting to him what he should say or how he should answer is another method for engaging him in conversational situations. For example the teacher may say to John:

John, ask Mary: "What did you do today?"

John asks Mary the question using the very words which the teacher has given him. The teacher then directs the answer by saying:

Mary, tell John: "I went shopping and bought a hat."

Mary answers by using the very words which the teacher has given her.

This same conversation can then be practiced by several other sets of students who use the same question and answer.

From this kind of conversation the teacher may proceed to a more complicated form in which he indicates what he wants the student to say but does not supply the actual words. For example:

John, ask Mary what she did in school today.

In this kind of guided conversation John will be required to manipulate the verb and the word order so that he can phrase a proper question for Mary to answer. Mary will be told:

Mary, tell John that you went to the French Club after school.

In this kind of guided answer Mary, too, will have to show that she knows how to handle the language.

After the students have learned to formulate questions and answers and can handle these small conversations well, the teacher can show them how to expand the drill and learn additional verb forms by using them in natural situations.

For example, the dialogue has been directed as follows:

Teacher: John, ask Mary where she is going today.

John to Mary: Where are you going today?

Teacher to Mary: Tell John that you are going to the store.

Mary to John: I am going to the store.

Teacher to John: Tell me that Mary says that she is going to the store today.

John to Teacher: Mary says that she is going to the store today. Or: She says that she is going to the store today.

After the first time, the directed sentence, "She says, that she is going to the store today," addressed to the teacher, can follow every set of questions and answers. In this way the student is learning to handle several additional forms of the verb in a natural conversational context.

Application

To give purpose and direction to language instruction it is imperative that the student use, in plausible situations, the language he has acquired. Since the language the student has been practicing and manipulating refers to some aspect of real life situations, he should be able to apply what he has learned by engaging in meaningful conversation with the other students of the class. The student should be encouraged to show his ingenuity by varying the order in which he asks his questions. The student who responds can use any number of responses since he has been taught several answers in the variety of chain drills in which he has engaged. The imaginative student will make use of previously learned material as well as the language he has recently acquired in the current unit of work.

At the beginning of the study of a foreign language, the teacher cannot expect the learner to be very creative. However, he can be encouraged to try to remember and use as much of what he has learned as possible. He can be expected to attempt a certain amount of originality by rearranging the elements and applying them to new situations. Even the beginning student can be taught how to show ingenuity. For instance, after asking the same question, "Is this a chair?" and pointing to the same chair many times, the teacher can demonstrate how to vary the technique by asking the question, "Is this a chair?" while pointing to a table. The answer does not require the use of a negative construction, if it has not yet been taught. It can be a simple "It is a table."

Given the opportunity, most students enjoy using their imagination. The leaders usually come up with new combinations which the others attempt to imitate.

It is up to the teacher to create situations where the student can use all the language at his command and to show him how he can demonstrate his inventiveness without ever resorting to asking the teacher, "How do you say this in French?"

There are many simulated life situations in which students can engage. Two students can be called up to the front of the room to pretend that they are meeting in the street. Their conversation can concern any topic they feel capable of conversing about. The one condition which must be observed is that only forms which have been studied and which are correct will be acceptable. Another real life conversation could take place on the telephone. This can be a two- or a three-way conversation.

There should be some form of free conversation every day in the foreign language classroom. This serves many useful purposes. It gives the students the chance to use the language which they have learned in natural situations. It gives the imaginative, enthusiastic student the chance to show off what he knows. He usually sets the example which other students try to imitate. Even the less aggressive student can be given the incentive to try to engage in conversation. It serves as a review since it causes the student to reach back in his memory for language which he has learned and may want to use. Free conversation keeps interest alive. It varies the routine of the class period. Students begin to like to perform as they get used to getting up on their feet and speaking to one another. They feel confident because they are not asked to use language of which they are unsure.

Culminating Projects

The study of a unit should come to a close with a culminating project in which the whole class takes part. The central theme of the project should coincide with the objectives of the unit.

It may take the form of a dramatization with as many characters as possible. It may be necessary to have two or three casts of characters and two or three re-enactments to include every member of the class. The important thing is that every member of the class must feel involved in performing and showing that he has learned what the unit set out to teach him.

The culminating activity may take the form of a round table discussion, with a panel of experts and questions from the floor. The panel of experts can be changed once or twice if necessary.

It may take the form of a social gathering where people speak to each other and then walk over to join other groups. For the older students paper cups of soda can give the atmosphere of a cocktail party. The teacher must circulate and eavesdrop to see that the language being used is correct.

There are many units which lend themselves to culminating projects like guessing games, charades, riddle solving, etc. Of course these will have to suit the age-level of the student. The teacher can get many ideas for games from the TV programs in which games are played.

The test for mastery is the ability to do coordinated and unified activities having life values. There is no better way to giving the student the feeling of accomplishment than by providing the opportunity for him to coordinate and put to use the material he has been learning. Well-planned and carefully executed culminating projects after each unit provide meaningful, purposeful activity and will engender enthusiasm for more language learning.

SUGGESTED READINGS:

Bloomfield, Leonard, *Language* (New York, Holt, Rinehart and Winston, 1945).

Brooks, Nelson, *Language and Language Learning: Theory and Practice* (New York, Harcourt, Brace & World, 1960).

Dale, Edgar, "The News Letter," Bureau of Educational Research and Science, Ohio State University, Columbus, Ohio 43210.

Northeast Conference on the Teaching of Foreign Languages, "Foreign Language Teaching—Ideals and Practices," Reports of the Working Committees, 1964.

O'Connor, Patricia, "Modern Foreign Languages in High School: Pre-Reading Instruction," Bulletin 1962 (OE-27000), U.S. Department of Health, Education, and Welfare, Office of Education, Washington, D.C. 20202.

Rivers, Wilga M., *The Psychologist and the Foreign Language Teacher* (Chicago, University of Chicago Press, 1964).

5
GRAMMAR THROUGH
PERFORMANCE—
THE PATTERN DRILL

- To develop *vocal* behavior in the student the teacher needs to use *oral* procedures.
- The pattern drill possesses all the features for teaching the structures through the sounds of a language.
- A pattern drill is constructed on a grammatical analysis of a linguistic and not a written feature of the language.
- Pattern drills are classified according to the function they perform.
- Pattern drills help the student to acquire insight, control, and proficiency.
- Pattern practice requires a lively interplay between teacher and student.
- Pattern drills are used in the classroom and the language laboratory.

Every craftsman needs the proper tools with which to do a specific job. The teacher also must analyze the task to be done and select the tool which will help him do that job well. The teacher needs to use verbal, linguistically-based tools in order to develop verbal behavior in the student. He cannot hope to teach the student to comprehend and to speak by requiring him to read. Nor can he expect the student to develop vocal fluency by being taught how to write. Neither will the student learn to speak by being subjected to memorizing lists of words and rules of grammar. The only way in which a student will learn to develop fluency and accuracy in comprehending and speaking is by hearing and speaking.

One tool designed to help the teacher produce aural and verbal activity in the student is the pattern drill. This drill is an instructional device based on what the structural linguist knows about language and what the psychologist knows about learning. The pattern drill was designed as an instrument for the foreign language teacher to use to teach the sound and structure of the language.

This kind of drill is not reserved solely for use with the newer courses of instruction nor with the latest electronic equipment. It can be used by all teachers of language no matter which language they are teaching, and no matter what other materials they are using. It can be adapted for use with the traditional textbook (see page 168) as well as for use with audio-lingual courses of instruction, is as useful in the classroom without the language laboratory as it is in the one with the language laboratory, and can be used on all levels of language instruction from courses in the elementary school up to the most advanced courses in the college or university.

DEFINITION OF THE PATTERN DRILL

The pattern drill is an oral exercise designed to enable the student to acquire verbal control over a grammatical construction. This is accomplished by providing sufficient repetitions of the motif of the exercise in a number of similar contexts so that the linguistic pattern emerges.

CHARACTERISTICS OF THE PATTERN DRILL

1. *The pattern drill presents the student with one difficulty at a time.* The drill is constructed to make the student dwell on one specific point until a pattern emerges which is recognized and thoroughly learned. Psychologists say that experimentation shows that optimum learning is achieved by single-step emphasis.

2. *Grammar is taught inductively.* This is the most important function of the pattern drill. The student is trained to search for structure. If he is alerted to look for an element in a pattern

he is very apt not only to find it but also to remember it. The drill helps the student to assimilate the rule through usage and function. He learns grammar through performance. He accepts the language as it is and not as someone says it ought to be. Grammatical terminology is reduced to a minimum.

3. The pattern drill, by dint of practice and repetition, *teaches the student to produce an automatic oral response.* It trains the ear and helps the student to link sound with meaning. Grammatical function is related to sound and after numerous repetitions correct language begins to sound right and incorrect language begins to sound wrong.

4. Pattern drills *resemble normal speech.* They are constructed on small segments of language in which meaning is evident because it is taught in context. Each nuance of meaning is taught in a separate drill. The student acquires a stock of basic expressions which are on tap for immediate recall and use. The pattern drill takes the student from an imitative, dependent response to an independent answer which is usable when the occasion arises.

5. The pattern drill *is economical.* It saves the time of both the teacher and the student. The teacher can drill orally as many as twenty sentences in five minutes with the entire class participating and benefitting. An exercise of the same length would probably take each individual student six times as long to write if given as a homework assignment; an equal amount of class time would be expended the next day for correction. If the teacher decides to correct the assignment outside of class, many additional hours of his time will be spent on that task. Since probability of error is low in a pattern drill, correction time is negligible.

Every student can benefit from the whole amount of time which is allotted to drill by participating either actively or silently in every aspect of the pattern drill. He spends little or no time waiting for some other student to answer. Since the student's responses are almost always correct he is not spending time on work which has to be unlearned or redone because of errors.

6. *The pattern drill provides immediate correction.* The in-

formation is given at the moment when it is of greatest interest to the student. The crucial time for him to know that what he has said is correct or incorrect is right after he has said it. If he knows that what he has said is correct, he can continue performing along the same lines. If what he has said is wrong, he is alerted and given the correct response.

The pattern drill provides the reinforcement necessary to "fix" the correct response. It does not permit the student to perpetuate or reinforce his error.

7. *The pattern drill seeks to perfect sound as well as structure.* It trains the student to know how to say as well as what to say. Pronunciation, intonation, and rhythm are as much a part of the drill as are the grammatical structures. The sonorities of the language are practiced along with the mechanisms of verb endings, word order, agreement of adjectives, etc., until both aspects, melody and construction, blend and become habit.

8. *The pattern drill teaches for transfer of knowledge.* It starts by teaching the initial understanding of structure. It then continues the process by developing new language habits and proficiency in the use of this learned material. The student having gained insight into structure is then guided to transfer what he has learned to other similar situations.

9. *The pattern drill is a flexible instrument* and, unlike the printed exercise, can be quickly adjusted to meet the situation of the moment. The success of the pattern depends on the interplay between teacher and student. It may not suit all students at all times. However, the astute teacher, because he, as well as the student, is involved in the action, will sense the need to adjust the drill on the spot so that it accomplishes the ends for which it was intended.

10. *The pattern drill keeps the class active.* It injects a lively tempo into the lesson. It is administered with a rhythmic beat. Every student is participating out loud or silently mouthing while some other members of the class are participating.

11. *The pattern drill keeps the class together.* The student must be alert, giving his undivided attention to hear what is being said so that he can perform correctly. Each cue is given just once.

During the oral drill there is no need for books, notebooks, papers, and all the other clutter on the student's desk which can divert his attention from what is going on in the class. The well-designed pattern drill eliminates the need for questions from individual students about structures, and their forms and functions. The pattern drill can also be used with great effectiveness at those times when the teacher needs to "pull the class together again."

12. *The pattern drill uses familiar vocabulary.* The drill is primarily intended to reinforce and manipulate structure rather than to build vocabulary. Learning new vocabulary while learning to control a linguistic pattern presents the student with too many problems at one time. His entire attention and effort is concentrated on controlling the pattern and developing proficiency in using it.

After a structure has become familiar it may then be used in a pattern drill for teaching new vocabulary. The situation to avoid is a pattern drill which attempts to teach new structure and new vocabulary at the same time.

13. *The pattern drill is easy enough for every student* of the class to do successfully. He is guided to the right answer by being given several examples which he mimics before he is requested to participate. After the exercise begins the pattern is repeated many times and those who are not ready to respond with the first sentence have several other chances to perform when they "catch on." They are not left behind simply because they could not begin with the rest of the class.

Since the correct response is given immediately after the student's response, those who started by giving incorrect answers have the opportunity to correct their errors. They can then continue along with the rest of the class and acquire the correct form by performing.

HOW TO CONSTRUCT PATTERN DRILLS

The construction of pattern drills requires careful grammatical and linguistic analysis of the items to be studied. The drills must be so constructed as to give the student habit-forming practice which will lead to correct performance in the foreign language. This practice will call his attention to pronunciation, intonation, linking, and the relationship of these phenomena of sound to their grammatical function or syntax.

In the construction of a pattern drill it is important to become aware of how the grammar of the spoken form of the language differs from the grammar of the language as it is written. Problems of pronunciation differ from problems of spelling. These must be considered separately and treated differently. The oral drill will concentrate on the grammar of the language as it is spoken.

For example: In French *il regarde* and *ils regardent* do not present the same difficulties in sound as they do in spelling. Since the *e* of *regarde* and the *ent* of *regardent* are both silent as is the *s* of *ils*, the sound of both of these verb forms is exactly alike even though they look quite different when written.

In Spanish the word *vivo* when pronounced sounds quite differently from the way it looks. The *v* sounds more like *b* than *v* to the ears of an English-speaking student.

Each language has its own linguistic system and no two languages have exactly the same systems. Therefore the construction of a pattern drill, which is by definition an oral exercise, must be based on the knowledge of the spoken system of the foreign language. The drill can only be effective if it is built on an accurate grammatical analysis of a linguistic and not a written feature in the foreign language. This feature to be studied and drilled must be identified and isolated.

For example, one may decide to treat object pronouns in French. Before constructing any drill, the topic must be examined and divided into all its elements. There are two kinds of object pronouns, direct and indirect. Only one of these should be drilled at a time. Suppose the choice is made to teach direct object pronouns first. These are then subdivided into all the possible elements of direct object pronouns. They are *le, l', la,* and *les* as well as *me, te, se, nous* and *vous.* For each of these a separate pattern drill is to be designed.

The drill for the pronoun *le* may be treated in the following way. The teacher lists as many as twenty sets of sentences in which masculine nouns become direct object pronouns:

> *Je vois le professeur. Je le vois.*
> *Je vois le garçon. Je le vois,* etc.

The drill for the direct pronoun *la* will require a similar treatment using feminine nouns which will become direct object pronouns:

> *Je regarde la fenêtre. Je la regarde.*
> *Je regarde la porte. Je la regarde,* etc.

The drill for the plural is constructed the same way:

> *Je regarde la porte et la fenêtre. Je les regarde.*
> *Je regarde la porte et le bureau. Je les regarde.*
> *Je regarde le bureau et le crayon. Je les regarde,* etc.

Before tackling the pattern drill for indirect object pronouns this topic, too, will have to be divided into its elements. Each element will require a separate drill. Only after all of these have been presented to and mastered by the student should the two types of object pronouns, direct and indirect, be combined and presented. Prior to constructing any drill, the entire topic of direct and indirect object pronouns will have to be analyzed and divided into all the possible elements of sequence. Each instance of sequence will require a separate drill. There will be one drill for *me le,* another for *me la,* still another for *me les* and so on until every combination of direct and indirect object pronoun has been presented and drilled. The use of these pronouns in imperatives, in negatives, and in compound tenses will require separate drills.

The study of verbs should be treated in the same way. Each person of the verb should be developed by a separate pattern drill thoroughly taught and drilled before going on to another person of the verb. Only after each person has been taught should a drill be constructed where all the forms appear together. A pattern drill should be simple and rigid so that the motif is not hidden in a clutter of unnecessary verbiage, but emerges bold and clear.

The length of each drill can vary depending on the needs of the student. It must be long enough for the student to "catch on" and master the pattern but not so long that it becomes boring. However, it is suggested that the shortest drill include at least eight variants. The whole approach must be systematic. There should be a progression from the simple to the complex.

TYPES OF PATTERN DRILLS

There are several types of drills. The objective of the lesson will determine which type of drill one will use. Many names have been given to the many varieties of pattern drills. Various linguists codify them differently. Some have divided pattern drills into as many as thirty categories. All the available classifications can be reduced to three types according to the function they perform.

There is one type of drill which requires the student to do nothing but repeat exactly what he hears. This is the *repetition drill*. There is another type in which the student is required to place a given clue in the proper position in the sentence. This is the *replacement* or *substitution drill*. In the third type, the *transformation drill*, the student must change the form of one structure to another form.

The Repetition Drill

The foreign language student depends on the teacher to teach him what to say and how to say it. He cannot say what he has not been taught to say, nor can he say what he has not heard being said. The repetition drill is used to present a segment of language to the student. Before he can be expected to create a similar structure he will have to hear the form several times, repeat, imitate, and understand what he is to do. The repetition drill, unless it is used purely for perfecting pronunciation, should precede the replacement or transformation drill.

In the repetition drill the teacher furnishes the example,

then the student repeats and mimics. As with every other drill, dialogue, or narrative, the teacher must use every device possible for establishing meaning. Mimicry without comprehension is speech production but not language learning.

For example, if a teacher of Spanish wishes to teach a lesson dealing with the position of adjectives he might construct the following drill.

Tengo un libro blanco.
Tengo un libro rojo.
Tengo un libro grande.
Tengo un libro francés, etc.

Before attempting to elicit any information from the student as to the position of the adjectives the teacher would pronounce each sentence as he uses various devices to make the students understand which book he is describing. When he is sure that the students understand what he is saying he will repeat the sentences one at a time and indicate that he wants the class to repeat each one after him exactly as they hear it. He will engage the class in this repetitive activity, by full chorus, half chorus, and individuals until he is sure that everyone can properly repeat these structures.

This kind of mimicry accomplishes several important things for the student. Only after he has engaged in successful repetition should he be asked to manipulate the structures he has learned to pronounce.

Successful repetition of the exercise described above shows the student the pattern of the normal position of adjectives in Spanish. Presented with sufficient examples and guided by the teacher, the student will come to the conclusion that adjectives in Spanish are placed after the word they describe. After having heard and reproduced many, many examples of this phenomena himself the sound will help "fix" this structure in his ear and mind. It will begin to sound right to him and he will be carried by the sound to create the right form for himself. We have all had the experience of being able to repeat structures which we have heard many times in verses or songs simply because we have been carried along, often unconsciously, by the sound of these words and phrases in our "mind's ear." The television and radio commercials constantly make use of this principle.

Another factor of importance in the repetition drill is that it teaches the student how to pronounce and intone the sentences he is learning. He may also see gestures and movements which help make the language more natural and meaningful. The problem of linking, a very important feature of spoken language which can present serious interference to comprehension, occurs in the normal course of pronunciation and is absorbed in the practice exercise. The student is taught to handle the construction as a whole with fluency.

The repetition drill provides the teacher with the occasion to concentrate on teaching meaning with sound. He can focus his entire attention and effort on getting the student to understand and to mimic.

Only after having achieved these two goals should the student be asked to manipulate the structure in subsequent drills. Because he will already understand the meaning of the language involved in the manipulative drills and because he will have achieved fluency in pronouncing these structures, the substitution or transformation drills which will follow the repetition drill will be more meaningful and more easily performed.

The Simple Substitution Drill

The simple substitution drill is characterized by the fact that the student is required to replace one segment of language by another segment. The rest of the pattern remains the same. The segment changes and with it naturally, will come some change in meaning. The repetition drill in Spanish above (see page 60) will change to a replacement drill when the teacher, instead of giving the whole utterance himself, asks the student to make the required changes.

In the Spanish example above the student would be given the pattern *tengo un libro blanco* and instructed to insert in their proper place the adjectives they will hear. The teacher utters the word *rojo* and the student supplies the whole sentence *tengo un libro rojo*. Then the teacher utters the next adjective *grande* and again the student supplies the whole sentence inserting the given adjective in the correct position in the sentence.

Before every pattern drill the student is given explicit directions and one or two examples so that he will know exactly what to do. After sufficient practice and drill, these instructions can be given in the foreign language.

The substitution or replacement drill can be used on all levels of language instruction from the simplest constructions to the most complex. A drill could be constructed for teaching a simple concept such as gender. A drill in German might be:

> *Hier ist die Wand*
> *Tür*
> *Mann,* etc.

A drill on a more advanced level could require the student to replace a verb and put it in its proper place in the sentence.

Such a drill in Spanish might be:

> *Juan trabaja en la ciudad*
> *viaja*
> *canta,* etc.

A drill on a very advanced level in French concentrates on a construction which presents several problem areas to the English-speaking student: the use of the subjunctive after *avant que* and the addition of the *ne* in the subordinate clause.

> *Je partirai avant qu'il ne pleuve*
> *avant qu'elle ne vienne*
> *avant qu'il ne parte,* etc.

The Progressive Substitution Drill

When the student has learned, in several drills, all the elements of a topic and can handle them fluently and well, a drill can be constructed in which the word he is asked to replace shifts its position from sentence to sentence. This drill is more complicated than the simple substitution one. It requires the student to make replacements with structures he has learned and it obliges him, in addition, to remember the order of the patterns as they shift from sentence to sentence. This kind of drill is used for developing the memory span of the foreign language student.

A progressive substitution which might follow the teaching of first, second, and third conjugation verbs in Spanish could be:

> Juan trabaja en la ciudad.
> > vive
> Juan vive en la ciudad.
> > en Madrid
> Juan vive en Madrid.
> Pedro
> Pedro vive en Madrid.
> > come
> Pedro come en Madrid.
> > en el hotel
> Pedro come en el hotel.

The substitution drill has all the advantages of the replacement drill and several more. By learning to replace just one segment in the drill by many variants, the student acquires oral control over that many more structures. He learns to manipulate language by adding what he already knows to what he is in the process of learning. One basic phrase may be arranged to elicit a great many responses. The combination of two or three substitution drills can give the student control over hundreds of sentences. For instance a substitution drill on a pattern of first conjugation verbs added to a pattern of prepositional phrases of place added to a pattern drill of expressions of time would, by combination and permutation, add up to several hundred usable sentences.

The Transformation Drill

This drill, as its name suggests, requires the student to transform one construction into another. These exercises can be used on all levels of instruction wherever the student is asked to change a given form. This can refer to verbs, adjectives, parts of sentences, etc. For instance, the drill may ask the student to change the subject of the verb and make all the appropriate changes in the sentence.

For example, a verb drill in German could be:

Ich habe einen Bleistift.
Du (hast)
Er (hat), etc.

Or it may involve changing a noun to a pronoun. A drill in French might be:

Je vois le professeur. Je le vois.
Je vois le garçon. Je le vois.
Je vois le livre, etc. *Je le vois,* etc.

Although transformation drills are very useful on every level, they are especially well-suited to the advanced level of language instruction. Well-designed drills can require students to perform in very complex situations. For instance, there are drills which ask the student to combine two short sentences into one long sentence. In the process the student needs to make the necessary structural and syntactical changes which will result in one complete, correct sentence. It may mean using the subjunctive in the dependent clause, or using present participles in place of one of the short sentences, or using relative pronouns to connect the two thoughts expressed in both sentences.

For instance, a drill in French might ask the students to combine two short sentences like:

Jean patinait. Il s'est cassé la jambe.

The new sentence would be:

En patinant Jean s'est cassé la jambe.

One in Spanish might ask the student to preface each sentence of the drill with the words *siento que.* This would require the use of the subjunctive in the dependent clauses.

> *lo dice*
> *Siento que lo diga.*
> *nos han pedido*
> *Siento que nos hayan pedido.*

The construction of pattern drills for use in the language laboratory (see page 83) resembles the types we have described above except that they are recorded on tape. Because there is no teacher present to correct errors as soon as they are made, provision for correction must be made on the tape. This takes the form of recording the correct response after the student has given his own response. For example, the student is asked to substitute the pronouns for the nouns in the following pattern drill in Spanish.

> *El me dió el libro. Me lo dió.*
> *El me dió el lapiz. Me lo dió.*
> *El me dió el dinero. Me le dió*, etc.

The recording on the tape would be:

(Model's voice giving the first example)
El me dió el libro. Me lo dió.
El me dió el lapiz. (Pause for student's response)

(Model's repetition)
Me lo dió. (Pause for student's correction)

In the second pause the student compares what he has said to the response on the tape. If he is wrong the pause gives him the time to correct his response. If he is correct, the pause gives him the chance to reinforce the correct response by saying it a second time.

In writing out the tapescript in preparation for the recording, every word must be written out and all the pauses must be indicated by a sign. The tapescript for the exercise above will look like this:

El me dió el libro. Me lo dió.
El me dió el lapiz. # Me lo dió. #
El me dió el cuaderno. # Me lo dió. #, etc.

The substitution and transformation drills give the student control through automaticity, over syntactical patterns, idiomatic structures, and basic sentence structure special to the foreign language which he is studying. Developing automaticity and fluency in such areas as verb forms, and agreement of adjectives or past participles, can best be achieved correctly by the systematic use of carefully planned manipulative exercises.

Although the pattern drill is an oral drill it can become a useful tool for instruction of writing. When the student is learning to write the foreign language (see Chapter 7—Writing) the basic design of the various types of pattern drills can then be used for written exercises.

The construction of a pattern drill is based on a knowledge of linguistic phenomena special to each language. What applies to one language does not apply to another. The section, *How To Construct Pattern Drills,* can only deal in the most general terms with this complicated subject.

It is hoped that what has been written here will serve to give the teacher some insight into the mechanics of drill construction. It is further hoped that his curiosity has been piqued sufficiently to make him go to the books on linguistics which have been written on the language that he is teaching. There he will see how the principles apply specifically to what he is endeavoring to do in his classroom.

APPLICATION

No matter how well the student repeats or manipulates a pattern drill we cannot be sure he has learned unless he has gained insight into the pattern, and through it into a generalization. Only then can this knowledge become the foundation for more language learning. Robert Politzer calls this acquiring "building stones." This generalization is remembered best if it is discovered by the students themselves and expressed by them.

They will learn to generalize if the teacher helps them focus their attention on the problem to be solved by devices such as:

- Preparing them for generalization by these kinds of questions: "What do you notice in the following sentences?" Or: "Why do you think the following sentences are so similar?"
- Presenting parallel construction of many examples of the structure under study. No one can come to a generalization from one example and it is easier to see a situation if the examples are very similar.
- Emphasizing by use of gestures, visuals, or voice tone those phrases in each example from which the generalization will be drawn.

Grammatical terminology is not important, and in fact, is to be avoided. If the generalization is expressed in terms of usage or function it will be more meaningful to the students. If the students do not perceive the motif and cannot formulate a generalization, the teacher should formulate it for them. Here, too, the language of function is preferred to the technical language of the grammarian. Therefore before the teacher leaves the pattern drill he should be sure that the generalization expressed either by the student or by himself is understood by all the students in the class.

Pattern drills must not only serve to give the student insight and control over linguistic patterns but they must also serve as a means of developing his proficiency in the use of that pattern. No matter how well the pattern drill teaches or drills the student in syntactical constructions, it becomes valuable only when the student can put to use what he has learned. Every drill must terminate in purposeful activity by the student in which he performs by utilizing his recently acquired knowledge.

This may take the form of short dialogues in which the questions that are asked by the teacher require an answer in which the newly learned language must be used. A drill in which the student has been taught to replace nouns by pronouns should end in a series of questions wherein the student responds by using pronouns in his answer. A drill in which the student has learned the various tenses of a verb must include a terminal activity in which the student uses the verb in various contexts.

Tense recognitional words should help the student determine the form of the verb which must be used. Including such words as "yesterday," "everyday," "tomorrow," "all last year," first in the drill and then in the questions, combines structure with contextual usage.

The pattern drill is not an end in itself, but a means to an end. That end is performance by the student in real life situations.

ADMINISTERING THE PATTERN DRILL

The written pattern drill can be compared to the score of a musical selection. The score must be properly rehearsed, and the notes must become sounds if the piece is to be enjoyed as music. The pattern drill must also be properly rehearsed, and the written words must become sounds if they are to become useful language. Just as with a piece of music, the pattern drill must acquire tempo and rhythm as well as sound.

As we have indicated above (see page 24), oral performance can best be done smoothly and without unnecessary interruptions by establishing a system of hand gestures and body motions. These act as lines of communication between the conductor and the performers. Each gesture or motion elicits a different kind of performance from the student. Once established, this sign language makes drill procedure easy to administer.

One signal is needed to tell the class to listen, another to tell them to repeat, and still another to indicate that they are required to speak, respond, or answer. It is helpful to have a gesture which tells part of the class to mouth the sounds while the other part of the class is saying them aloud. This keeps everyone participating, some actively, some silently.

Some kind of motion is necessary to indicate that one-half of the class is to perform or that only one row is to act. The number of fingers upheld can indicate how many consecutive repetitions are desired. Students need not be called upon by name. Pointing to a student means that he is requested to answer. If these signals are not clearly differentiated and understood, the pattern practice will become disorganized and undisciplined and the result will be frustrating to both teacher and student.

The drill begins by having the teacher give the instructions clearly so that everyone knows what is required of him. The teacher follows this up by giving at least two examples. This eliminates the necessity of questions and interruptions by the students. The examples are given at normal speed and the signal for the class to join in is given after the second example. As the teacher is administering the drill he is moving around the room. The drill always starts with full chorus and moves to half chorus, then to rows or groups, i.e., all boys, all girls, all blondes, etc. The drill moves to the individual student only after sufficient practice has taken place by the whole and various parts of the class.

As seen in the sections on substitution and transformation drills, most drills are made up of a model, a cue, and a response:

The boy is good	(model)
bad	(cue)
The boy is bad	(response)

The teacher pronounces the model. He sets the pace of the drill by giving the model at normal speed and pronouncing the cue directly after enunciating the model. He signals for a response immediately after the cue and keeps the drill moving along by not permitting the class to dawdle over the response. He establishes a rhythm between model and cue, and between cue and response which he tries not to break until the drill has been completed.

However, the drill must be interrupted if the response is incorrect. The correction is made immediately by the teacher who calls for one or two repetitions of the corrected response and then continues the drill reestablishing the original tempo. Mistakes in pronunciation are considered incorrect responses and the drill is interrupted to correct those, too, as soon as they are detected.

Incorrect responses by individuals are treated the same way. When it is obvious that the student is unable to answer correctly, it is efficient for the teacher to give the correct response immediately. The student then repeats the corrected response.

The teacher may call for a choral repetition of the corrected response if he thinks that the class will benefit from it.

The cues in a pattern drill need not always be verbal. Sometimes they can be pictures which are presented after the model has been enunciated. The response must include the word suggested by the picture. Sometimes the cue can be a gesture. For instance a negative response may be requested by shaking the head as if to say "no." An affirmative response may be suggested by shaking the head as if to indicate "yes." Sometimes the cues may be real objects. These are held up in place of the spoken cue and the names of these cue objects are incorporated by the student in his response.

Only one new point is taught at a time, and that is drilled until it is assimilated. The teacher does not move on to a new point until the old one is understood by everyone.

When the teacher moves around the room while conducting the drill, he needs both arms free to use in gesturing. He must not be encumbered by a book or a notebook. His drills should be written out on small cards which he can hold in one hand and consult very unobtrusively whenever necessary. He never speaks with the students. He speaks first, and they imitate or respond after him. The teacher gestures after the cue is given, not before.

The transition from one drill to another or from a drill to questions and answers should be smooth and without a lag. The entire lesson should be well articulated to keep it moving and to keep the student alert and active all through the period.

The pattern drill cannot be repetition alone. It must include questions and answers and chain drills (see pages 43–48). The sensitive teacher will know when to vary the procedure and when to return to the pattern drill if there is need for further drilling.

BEWARE!

Pattern practice is predicated on repetition and correction. The drill can be very effective if it is used properly. In the hands of a knowing, sensitive teacher the pattern drill is efficient and makes for pleasurable learning. The foreign language lesson is lively, varied, and interesting. When mishandled, the drill can be boring, wasteful, and even harmful to learning.

Mere practice does not make perfect. One can practice error as well as perfect forms. Practice to be effective requires an excellent model to imitate. One cannot practice mediocrity and come out with excellence.

Repetition does not insure learning. Unrelenting, unremitting repetition becomes boring and distasteful. It may cause the student to avoid the exercise mentally or physically. He may actually absent himself from the classroom, or he may escape the repetition by not participating. He may even prevent others from participating by making a nuisance of himself.

Overlong repetition can be self-defeating when it causes fatigue. Fatigue in turn affects the student's ability to learn. Brains and muscles do not coordinate well when tired, even though the learner may have the best intention to pay attention and to participate in the lesson.

Poor, sloppy practice will result in poor, sloppy learning. A poorly designed drill which lacks cohesion cannot result in well-directed learning. An indifferent orchestra leader and apathetic performers cannot produce a perfectly executed and harmonious concert.

Imitation without understanding cannot result in useful knowledge. Thinking must be included somewhere in the repetitive drill if it is to produce information which will serve the learner in the future.

If one capitalizes on its strengths and avoids its pitfalls, the pattern drill properly organized and executed will reward both teacher and learner many times over for the time and effort that each contributes.

SUGGESTED READINGS:

Belasco, Simon, *Anthology* (Boston, Heath, 1961).

Diller, Edward, "The Nature of Linguistics in the Direct Method of Foreign Language Teaching," *Hispania*, Vol. 44 (March, 1961).

Hall, Robert A. Jr., *Linguistics and Your Language* (Garden City, N.Y., Doubleday, 1960).

Lado, Robert, "Linguistics and Foreign Language Teaching," *Language Learning*, Vol. 10 (March 1961).

Northeast Conference on the Teaching of Foreign Languages, "Current Issues on Language Teaching," Reports of the Working Committees, 1962.

Politzer, Robert L., *Teaching French—An Introduction to Applied Linguistics* (Boston, Ginn, 1960).

Politzer, Robert L., and Staubach, Charles, *Teaching Spanish—A Linguistic Orientation* (Boston, Ginn, 1960).

6

THE NEW TECHNOLOGY—
IMPLICATIONS FOR
FOREIGN LANGUAGE
INSTRUCTION

- The teacher must try to reach today's student through modern instructional materials.
- The audials can provide the teacher and student with a variety of native, spoken language.
- The instructional program of the school should determine the choice and use of the language laboratory.
- Visuals help the teacher encode as well as decode the language he is teaching. Authentic visuals give the student better concepts.
- The motion picture can bring the world to the student.
- Educational television can present important current events which relate to the foreign land and its people.
- Programmed instruction has a role to play in foreign language instruction.

THE TEACHER AND THE MODERN STUDENT

There are many questions which come to mind as we look at the students seated before us in our classroom. Who is that student who comes for foreign language instruction? Where does he come from before entering our classroom each day? Where is he going after he leaves us? What kind of world absorbs him? How can we keep him interested in what we are teaching him? How can we hope to make an impact on him which he will carry with him from the classroom to the world beyond our doors?

If we hope to reach the student who sits before us day after day, we must see him as he functions in his own world. There is much that interests and engages him; there is much he learns without the benefit of instruction by a teacher. If we are to reach and motivate him, it is obvious that we shall have to understand what he learns from in the world outside the classroom and make use of that information in our instruction.

The student who comes into our classroom was born in this electronic age and takes its achievements for granted. They are part of his life. He learned to tune in the television set in his home before he could speak, and when he could barely toddle over to the set. The radio is a constant companion in his room, on his walks and, when he is of age, in his car.

He no doubt has had a camera among his possessions since early childhood. He and his family have probably recorded many of their vacations on color film. In all likelihood he can handle the projector and the tape recorder better than we can. His is an audio and visual world. He socializes around a juke-box. His own collection of records is a source of pride and satisfaction to which he and his friends sing and dance and accompany themselves with the proper motions and gyrations. The world in which he lives, grows, and learns is alive with noise, color, and movement.

And in what kind of classroom atmosphere do we expect him to learn? What kind of fare do we offer him? The same four walls, the same book, the same voice of the same teacher day after day?

If we are competing with his active, pulsating world for his attention and interest it is obvious that we are giving ourselves an overwhelming handicap. The channels of communication through which our student learns are easily discernible. We cannot expect enthusiasm from our twentieth century student by closeting him in a mid-Victorian classroom where he can see little or no connection between the world he knows and the environment he encounters in our chamber of learning.

THE TEACHER AND THE NEW MEDIA

The Audials

The electronic inventions of our time are particularly well suited to helping the teacher teach. Never before in the history of education has the language teacher had so many instructional materials at his disposal with which to teach *spoken* language. In retrospect we realize that the textbook was a very inadequate tool for teaching a skill which depends so much on sound for the teaching and the learning. No book on phonetics, no matter how well written and no matter how exact, can make the proper noises for the student to hear and imitate. No written conversation can give the student the inflections, the emphasis, or the emotions which are part of the utterances.

We have noted that the first two aims of foreign language teaching are to produce students who can understand the foreign language when it is spoken and who can speak so that everyone who knows the language can comprehend. The most fluent and accurate teacher cannot present the student with the various kinds of spoken language he needs to hear if he is to become competent enough to understand everyone who speaks the foreign language. Learning to understand one teacher, even the native speaker, is not enough for he is limited by his own cadence, his particular choice of vocabulary, and his particular personal style. The student needs to hear many different people, many different voices, and many different styles.

If the student is to be trained to understand the foreign language he shall have to hear not only many voices but many voices of natives. He must comprehend all kinds of authentic speech such as that of children, grown-ups, men and women, and boys and girls.

The language teacher is in the fortunate position today of having much recorded material available through which he can invite a host of native guests into his classroom. The record, the sound tape, the film, the radio, and the television provide the instructor with a variety of native voices when they can be most useful to him in his lesson and for as long or as short a visit as he deems necessary. From the very first day of language instruction the student should be exposed to listening to voices other than his teacher's. Some portion of every class period should be devoted to listening to native speakers.

This aural material should be used in conjunction with the regular course work, be it textbook or otherwise. The teacher who fails to make room for experiences in the aural comprehension of a diversity of native voices in many different situations is depriving his students of the most important and valuable aspect of language learning.

As the student advances in the study of the language he will need to learn to understand the different levels of spoken language. He will need to understand the "man in the street," the porter, the taxi-driver, the waiter, the chambermaid, and the desk clerk. He will want to understand the language which he hears on radio or television, the sound track of the movie film, and the actors and actresses on the stage.

All of these are available to the interested language teacher. The best lecturers, singers, poets, political leaders, popular entertainers, sport figures, and movie stars who are of particular interest to our students can, with the flip of a switch, enliven our lessons and enthuse our language learners. Electronically we can keep the student in constant contact with authentic spoken language and develop in him the competency to understand it.

Intensive exposure to different levels of language as well as to different dialects should be reserved for the more advanced students. However, the less advanced ones will be amused to listen, from time to time, to very small samplings of regional speech patterns and colloquial language.

The record player and tape recorder should be recognized standard equipment in every language classroom. The greatest boon to the language teaching profession, and the most versatile teaching tool of this century is without a doubt the tape recorder. It not only permits the student to hear authentic speech, but it also gives him the opportunity to hear his own efforts after he has tried to imitate that speech. The tape recorder can be the best helpmate a language teacher ever had. Recorded tape never gets provoked by hearing errors. It never changes its intonation or emphasis. It never loses its voice or patience. It can provide the student with as much practice as he can endure. The tape recording can help the teacher teach and drill. It can provide the perfect model for imitation and be the perfect tutor.

The wise teacher is one who uses the tape recorder to assist him wherever possible. The tape recorder, with properly recorded drills (see page 65) can take over the burden of practice, repetition, and correction in the classroom, but it is in the language laboratory that it can help the teacher most. In the laboratory, the tape recorder, basic ingredient of all laboratories, helps the student to practice what has been taught him in the classroom.

The Language Laboratory

The language laboratory is an educational tool and not a prestige symbol. Unfortunately it has come to be used in some communities more for show than for instruction. It has become the most controversial tool ever produced for the language teaching profession. It does have its staunch advocates but it also has many opponents. When it is used well it can be a very efficient, useful instrument for learning. When poorly used it can become the most expensive white elephant a school can possess. It can also become the center of strife for the teacher as well as the community.

The choice of the name language laboratory was an unfortunate one since it gives one a false impression of its real purpose. A laboratory is usually a place where research or experimentation goes on. Nothing of that nature should take place in the normal course of events in the language laboratory. A better name would have been an electronic practice hall or an electronic study hall. This is the place to which a student goes for further practice with the language which he has been taught in the classroom. Here is where he has the opportunity to correct his errors of sound and structure and to develop control of the language he is studying.

Language laboratory has been defined as an installation of electro-mechanical equipment to facilitate language learning. There are many different kinds of laboratories with varying degrees of complexity ranging from simple tape recorders to very elaborate, fully-equipped carrels. Some even contain small screens which can receive closed-circuit television programs. Each year new kinds of laboratories appear on the market. The instructional potential of each type varies with the number of devices which are built into its design.

Language laboratories vary widely. The simplest provides facilities for listening to the spoken language. The student simply repeats what he hears. The more complex provides facilities for listening through activated headphones and responding through an attached microphone. This permits the student to listen to the model's voice on the tape and to hear himself as he is imitating. The most complex provides facilities for listening, responding, recording, and playback. Here the student is able to listen to the model's voice, to record as he responds, and to play back the tape so that he can compare his performance with that of the model's.

Even the most modest of language laboratories is an expensive item. Before purchase, in order to insure its chances for success, the administration of a school should give serious thought to several basic considerations.

One important question to consider is whether the teachers of the department want a language laboratory. One ingredient without which no language laboratory can ever succeed is the willing teacher. If the general consensus of opinion is that all the teachers of the department do not want a laboratory, it would be better to postpone or cancel its installation. A language laboratory cannot be used well if it is installed in the face of opposition or reluctance by the teachers of the department.

In such a situation the administration can begin a subtle campaign of indoctrination. Talks at departmental meetings by enthusiastic teachers from other schools, or by state supervisors, films showing the use of the language laboratory, and visits to other schools where it is used successfully, may bring a few members around to the point where they will want to try a laboratory. A few enthusiastic teachers may show the others the way. However, until such time as the administration can be assured that a good percentage of the teachers of the department are willing to use the laboratory it is better to do without it. A community which has invested thousands of dollars in equipment is likely to keep a watchful eye on it. The resentment that can build up over the abuse or nonuse of a laboratory can cause the foreign language teachers much grief and public resentment.

Another factor to consider is what the teachers of the department see as their objectives in language teaching. Do they concentrate on reading and translation? Then they will not be kindly disposed to putting forth the effort required to make effective use of the laboratory. Do they consider comprehension and speaking as their primary objectives? Do they feel that the student cannot get enough practice in the classroom to achieve these objectives with a considerable degree of accuracy and fluency? If they do, they will be willing to learn to operate "the hardware" to get at the instructional potentials of the laboratory.

The advantages of language laboratories are many:

- They provide each student with guided practice to reinforce his work in the classroom.
- They provide authentic native voices as consistent, untiring models.
- They provide a sense of privacy and confidence by means of the headphones or booths which encourage concentration on the lesson.
- They free the teacher to monitor, correct, and evaluate the individual's performance without taking time from the rest of the class.
- They provide tutorial or remedial service for the student who needs it.

The decision to install a laboratory must be the result of discussions which include teachers, technicians, and administrators.

One important question to be resolved and upon which will rest most of the pedagogic potential is the physical equipment of the laboratory. Such choices as separate practice rooms, electronic classrooms, mobile units, and labs which accommodate only half a class at a time must be examined very carefully. The needs of the student body and what the laboratory can do to enhance instruction must take precedence over all other considerations. The most expensive laboratory which contains all the gadgets that the construction engineer dreams of could turn out to be too complicated for good use and minimal maintenance. On the other hand the inexpensive laboratory which does not accomplish its function for teacher and student is a waste of that much money which could be better spent for classroom materials. Simplicity with maximum efficiency is the combination sought.

The type of school, the age of the student, and the organization of class rosters will all affect the efficacy of the installation as well as the problems of scheduling so that the maximum good can be derived by the maximum number of students. For instance, the separate room is better suited to a college or university where students can go to the laboratory in their free time as they would go to the library. This may be on a voluntary or assigned basis. In this scheme, the laboratory is under the supervision of a laboratory assistant who takes attendance and supplies the master tapes to the students. There is rarely any monitoring of performance in this kind of situation.

The *separate practice room* presents special problems when it is installed in the senior or junior high school. It cannot easily be used in free time as the student would use a library. Classes as a whole must be programmed for set times during the week. This presents an inflexible situation and the student must go to the laboratory when it is on his schedule even if he would have profited better from practice at another time during the week when the work being done in the classroom calls for such practice.

The *electronic classroom* presents a more flexible situation. This installation permits every classroom to become a practice room at the exact time when the teacher feels the student needs drill and practice most. Every desk can be quickly and easily converted into a listening post, either by raising desk tops (where the electronic equipment is installed underneath) or by plugging headphones into jacks at each student's desk. Some installations provide movable walls which can be raised or lowered between desks converting each location into a separate booth.

The advantages of the electronic classroom are obvious. The problem of scheduling is eliminated. Students can benefit from practice when it is most pertinent and for as long or short a period of time as is needed. The displacement of the student from his regular classroom with all the attendant physical and psychological problems are avoided.

The *mobile laboratory* which moves from classroom to classroom usually cannot make provisions for all the students to use the facilities at the same time. This is also true of the room which provides facilities for only half or part of the class. In these situations the class period must be divided into two parts. One half of the class uses the laboratory while the other half is engaged in some other work at their desks. They reverse roles during the second half of the period. The disadvantages of such a system are obvious.

Another question worthy of examination is what the department expects the laboratory to be able to do. Should the student be able to listen to the model and record his response so that he can compare it with that of the model? Or would it be sufficient to have him listen to the model and hear his response through activated headphones without recording? Should he record every period which he spends in the laboratory or only occasionally?

If the department wants the student to record every period so that he can compare his performance to the model's, an installation with recording facilities at each student's position will be required. If it is decided that only occasional recording and playback is necessary, a few rows of recording installations will be sufficient. It is not advisable to have a laboratory with no recording facility at all. At least one row should be equipped to take care of any contingency which may occur where recording is necessary.

The age of the student will determine how many recording and playback facilities will be necessary. The younger ones probably will not need as many as the older ones. The college students will probably profit more from playback if they have learned to be critical of their own speech than will the junior high school students.

The question of the console should be discussed. It is from the console that the teacher monitors the performance of the student. This is where the student gets correction and criticism or praise. It is from the console that the teacher can get to the individual student and give him his undivided attention, the kind of attention he cannot give him in the classroom. Some consoles provide only for one way communication. The teacher can hear the student but he cannot talk to him. Other consoles provide for two-way communication. Teachers can hear the students and talk to them. This is very essential for immediate correction and reinforcement. Some consoles not only provide teacher to student, but even student to student communication.

The placement of the console is another question to consider. Should it be in front of the room where the teacher can be viewed by all the students or should it be in rear where the teacher can observe the students but where they cannot observe him?

Every aspect of laboratory installation should be thoroughly examined and discussed from the physical as well as the pedagogical point of view and a decision should not be hasty. The faculty should not permit itself to be pressured into a decision by a clever salesman. Visits to other schools with various kinds of installations are very helpful. One school may be able to profit from the other's mistakes or successful experiences.

While the language laboratory is under discussion and consideration it would be advisable to have a few members of the department take a course in the use of the language laboratory at a nearby college or university, if that is available, or at a workshop or institute. Ideally each member should have such a course. Where this is not possible, a few well-informed teachers can instruct the others.

When the laboratory has been decided upon and installed all the members of the department should participate in several sessions with the salesmen on the physical operation of the equipment. Each teacher should then practice all the functions of the various parts of the installation alone, away from students and other members of the department. Sufficient practice with knobs and buttons and tape will give the teacher the confidence necessary for use with the class when the time comes.

The laboratory, no matter how shiny and impressive it is, and no matter how well it runs, is only as good as the materials which are used in it. A budget must be established for the purpose of obtaining materials. Having an expensive laboratory without sufficient well-prepared, properly recorded material is like owning a very expensive automobile which sits in the garage because the owner does not want to spend money for gasoline. A good laboratory will build up a library of a variety of good quality, recorded materials for all levels of instruction. Many departments have discovered that it requires a great deal of technical know-how plus well-qualified native speakers to make good recordings. Also, production of materials which begins with script writing and goes on to securing the right voices, rehearsals, recording sessions, and editing reviews, consume many hours of a teacher's time.

Unless there is professional engineering help available, the quality of the teacher-made recordings are often not of top calibre. Usually it is better to buy materials than to make them in the school.

The classroom is where the lesson is taught; the language laboratory is where the lesson is practiced until controlled. The student must be made aware of this. When the student is introduced to the laboratory he must be given instructions in the operation of the equipment. He should know how to handle it well. He should be impressed with the cost of the equipment and made to feel that he is fortunate to have a laboratory to help him practice his skills.

Why he is in the laboratory and what he is expected to do there must be made clear to him. His mere presence in the laboratory will work no magic formula. His performance in the classroom will reflect whether or not he has practiced well in the laboratory. His final grade should reflect classroom performance as it has been affected by laboratory practice. Classroom exercises directly related to laboratory practice should appear in every lesson and quiz.

The language laboratory has come under attack from many quarters. Examination of the criticism shows that where the laboratory was used properly for what it was intended, i.e., to provide the student with models of authentic, native speech with which he can practice material which was previously taught in the classroom, it has proven successful. However, where it was used poorly and for purposes other than those relating to oral performance, the results left much to be desired. The laboratory has proven to be a disappointment to the administration which expected that the possession of a laboratory would automatically improve the foreign language instruction of the school. This electronic facility is only as good as the materials which are used in it and the teacher who knows how to use these materials.

Experience shows that as the foreign language teaching

community becomes better acquainted with language laboratory installations and learns to use them well, their effect on student performance becomes more and more noteworthy.

Evaluation of the effectiveness of the language laboratory of a school should be a continuing procedure after the first year of its operation. It should relate to the instructional process as well as to the equipment. If the laboratory is not contributing to the foreign language program, the department should consider ways for improving its use. Again, these discussions should involve teachers, technicians and the administration. Some of the most valuable criticism will come from those who sit in the laboratory with the headphones on their ears. Although the students need not be present at the evaluation discussions, their opinions and suggestions should be solicited and submitted to the evaluation committees.

This continuing self-evaluation and subsequent self-improvement will make the difference between a language laboratory which is merely tolerated by students and teachers and used indifferently, and the one which is a functioning vital tool, and an indispensable adjunct to the foreign language instructional program of the school.

The Visuals

Sound alone is not language. The reproduction of sonorities alone cannot achieve comprehension. Language is not the noise which we make with our vocal apparatus. This noise becomes language only when it communicates ideas from one man to another. Men cannot understand each other even if they do make the same noises unless they attach the same meaning to the noises which they are making. This is also true of the written word. The designs of the letters of the word do not communicate meaning.

For instance the word "white" may conjure up two different thoughts to two different people. To the man who lives in certain parts of Africa, white connotes mourning and sadness. When he hears or sees the word, this is the meaning it has for him. The American knows white to be the color which belongs to brides and weddings and gladness. The sight or sound of the word has diametrically opposed effects on the African and the American.

The language teacher is involved in a multi-faceted task. Speech production is certainly a very important aspect of the instructional program but it is only part of the job which must be done. The language teacher must always be involved in relating language, spoken or written, to concept. This is one reason why translation is to be avoided. The translator can bring to the foreign language only those concepts which he has built up in his own language and culture.

Concepts are acquired by experiences, and by involving as many senses as possible in the learning process. Sight added to sound brings more comprehension than sound alone. A person knows very little about *quiche lorraine* by just hearing or seeing the word. He learns more about it by seeing the object itself and still more by inhaling its delicious aroma right from the oven. His experience is even more complete when he tastes this delicacy and feels its delicate texture on his tongue and in his mouth and throat. To those who have never seen or tasted *quiche lorraine* an unfeeling translation such as *custard cheese pie with bits of bacon* would make any gourmet cringe.

Naturally in a classroom it is rarely feasible to give the student experiences in which all his senses are involved, although the teacher should try to do this wherever possible. However, it is possible to bring visuals into the classroom. In the opinion of the author, in foreign language teaching where instruction is constantly involved in teaching new and strange phenomena, it is imperative that visuals be used when and wherever possible to help students develop better concepts. Better concepts and consequently better understanding of the language will result. This is the normal way in which language acquires meaning for all of us. From the very first days of our lives we have derived meaning from sounds by associating them with people and things around us.

Our students today are sophisticated viewers. They have been reared on pictures and are surrounded by them constantly. The quality is usually the best that can be obtained. The producers of posters, advertisements, magazines, films, and television programs spare no expense to supply the public with superb pictures. The student becomes a very sophisticated viewer at an early age. Even his own efforts make him very wise in the use of a camera.

If the new technology has given us a sophisticated, blasé student it has also provided the teacher with exceptional instructional devices. The visual material which is available to the foreign language teacher today has never been so beautiful, so bountiful, and so easy to use. The use of visuals for teaching is not new. Comenius in his *Orbis Picturis* at the beginning of the seventeenth century wrote about the usefulness of associating language with pictorial matter. However, the quality, quantity, and scope of visual materials have improved considerably since the days of Comenius. They have become very exciting to use and more instructional than they ever were.

The term *visual materials* includes many different items. Charts, graphs, flash cards, the chalkboard, and the textbook are all visual materials. The photograph, the color slide, the filmstrip, the motion picture, and the television are all classified as visuals, too. Each has a role to play in language teaching and each should be used carefully for what it can bring to the educational process. For the most part, charts, graphs, stick figures, flash cards, the chalkboard, and the textbook are best used for exercises and drills. They are used effectively for stimulating quick responses to material already learned. This kind of item is best used as a signal or a symbol to activate oral activity. After the student has practiced his response by reacting to the symbols, the teacher withdraws the signals and the student performs without them.

To initiate a language lesson by the use of stick figures is to render it colorless and lifeless. In order to differentiate one figure from the other, stick drawings become caricatures and portray stereotypes such as the Mexican who wears the sombrero or sits under the cactus, and the Frenchman who wears a beret.

For teaching authentic meaning, the teacher must resort to authentic pictorial materials. These visuals must be chosen so that they convey as fully as possible the experiential environment of the natives who speak the language under study. Every language has its roots in a specific culture. Vocabulary has its cultural implications. The visuals which the teacher uses must relate to that culture. If they do not, they are not providing the student with the background he needs for acquiring true comprehension of the sounds he hears. For instance, if we show our student a picture of an American farm as we teach him language which relates to the French farm we are giving him erroneous ideas of what a French farm is like. *La basse-cour* of a French farm must be seen to be fully comprehended.

Through the authentic visual the teacher is afforded the opportunity of teaching the language against the cultural background and not apart from it. Language comes alive. It helps the student see how what he is learning belongs to other human beings who may be much like him or very different from him.

It is here that the new technology has provided the teacher with the most stimulating teaching tools. Modern photography can produce beautiful pictures. The teacher who subscribes to foreign language periodicals can build a fine collection of authentic pictorial material by clipping out the large, good pictures which appear in the magazines.

Posters have never been more attractive and in addition to providing teaching material, they help to create the desired atmosphere in the foreign language classroom. The foreign newspapers with their advertisements, pictures, and headlines also provide arresting, interesting, and instructional visuals for use in a lesson and for display on the wall or a bulletin board.

The field of projected visuals, the slide in color taken of some aspect of the foreign land, provides the teacher with authenticity and beauty and images large enough to be seen by everyone in the class at the same time. If they happen to be slides which were taken by the teacher himself or someone he knows, there is the added dimension of personal enthusiasm.

The filmstrip requires a minimum amount of storage space and is easy to handle. It also supplies large pictures in color. These usually follow in some order so as to develop a theme or a motif. The new projectors make the showing of slides and filmstrips very easy. The remote control device on some machines permits the teacher to control the change of picture from any part of the room.

Authentic still pictures, projected and non-projected, not only provide the teacher with tools for encoding, for bringing meaning to the language which he is teaching, but they also provide him with the vehicle, par excellence, for decoding, and for eliciting information from the student to prove that he has understood what he has been taught. Students often can give correct answers to questions without comprehending what the question has asked or what they have said in their answers. Visual materials give the teacher the tools for proving comprehension without resorting to the use of English. Students can use details in a picture to answer questions by pointing, touching, or illustrating.

Still pictures, too, can provide the teacher with a tool for developing oral activity. A good picture can become the focus for conversations, dialogues, directed narratives, and descriptions.

The motion picture stands alone as the visual tool which can bridge distances and time and which can give the student the vicarious experience of an actual visit. It takes him to the foreign land where he sees for himself the cultural setting of the language which he is studying. He learns about the people and their way of life by an experience which is as close to first hand as he can get without actually going abroad. This the motion picture does better than any other instructional device.

The motion picture synchronizes sound and sight. An armchair voyage to the foreign land via motion picture can help the student get more authentic meaning from the language he is studying than almost any other instructional device. M. Jean Benoit-Levy, a director of some of the first educational films in France, said that the motion picture was the open window through which one could see all parts of the world.

The motion picture also can take the student to visit with people of today and yesterday. He sees them in their own native environment and they become more than mere names to him. He may also come to know some who are not well-known but who make up "the people" whose language he is learning. The teacher who neglects to give his students motion picture experiences in the foreign land is depriving him of the opportunity to get the fullest comprehension from the language he is studying.

The motion picture, however, has been used for other kinds of instructional purposes. Attempts have been made to teach grammar facts, structures, and phenomena of pronunciation. In these areas, in the opinion of the author, the motion picture film does not provide the student and the teacher with the flexibility which they need. The moving picture is a rigid tool which proceeds at a given speed until it has run its course. One cannot stop at any spot to dwell a little longer or to examine a little closer the point which has just been made in the film.

It is not easy to relocate on the film something which needs repeating or re-emphasis. In areas such as the teaching of structure or pronunciation there may be need for numerous consecutive repetitions of one item. It is not possible on motion picture film to turn small portions back and forth several times for such exercises.

For reteaching or re-emphasizing something in the middle of the film which apparently has not "taken hold" the first time, it is necessary to start the film all over again from the beginning. The teaching of pronunciation and grammatical structures need tools which are more flexible than the motion picture film. The sound tape which permits easy, numerous repetitions, accompanied by the appropriate visual material is much less rigid and will probably give the teacher more versatility and, therefore, more satisfaction.

Educational television is engaging the time and attention of many people. The television set has become an educational tool in countless schools today. As with any other instructional instrument, it is only as good as the material which is shown on the screen. The added hazard in television is that a poorly taught lesson affects many classes, not just one. Educational television is being used on closed and open circuits and on all levels of instruction from the elementary school to the college.

Since language learning requires meaningful presentation backed up by much practice, instruction by television presents a special problem in foreign languages. The effectiveness of the tele-lesson relies heavily on the follow-up procedures which should take place after the lesson has been presented. In some cases, usually with adolescent or adult students, this is left to the individual who uses a book or recorded materials to guide and help him with his practice. The conscientious grown-up with a discriminating ear may be able to do well by himself. The individual who needs guidance and correction does not fare as successfully.

Educational television is being used widely for teaching foreign language in the elementary schools (FLES). Thousands of children are starting their language education with a television teacher who gives them instruction twice or three times a week. The teacher in the classroom is usually responsible for conducting the necessary repetition and practice between tele-lessons. Where the follow-up practice is conducted by an interested teacher who has a good command of the language the television course can meet with success. However, when it is in the hands of a classroom teacher who has not had sufficient training in the foreign language or who is disinterested, the tele-lesson, excellent though it may be, will not produce the desired learning. It has been known to discourage the student from continuing with further language instruction.

The tele-lesson is even more inflexible than the motion picture film. Once presented, it is finished for all time. It cannot be recaptured for easy reuse by the classroom teacher. (Kinescopes and videotapes are not easily obtainable. The tapes are not easy to use in the average classroom.) The audio and visual materials which were used in the tele-lesson and through which the student made his first association with the new material are not available to the practice teacher who may want to use them for some re-teaching, or for review, or for re-emphasis.

The television course imposes an inflexible schedule on all those who are involved in the program. Lessons take place at scheduled times and all classes must take instruction whether they are ready for a new lesson or not. This lock-steps everyone, the bright and the not so bright, the one who has had sufficient practice and the one who has not had enough, and the one who has comprehended and the one who has not.

The television teacher cannot establish the empathy, or the interpersonal relationships with his students which are so necessary in foreign language instruction. Speech is psychological behavior. The dependence of the student on the teacher has already been discussed (see page 44). In the television situation student and teacher are very remote from one another. The friendly, personal rapport necessary for confidence in performance cannot be established between the two.

However, television can be used with great success for that which it is designed to do best. It can give the student a front seat near the stage where something interesting is taking place. It can supply the teacher with natural situations where the language is used. It can present good, current happenings. Television makes possible the viewing of celebrations, special occasions, dramatic performances, current events, and prominent personalities. This is the great strength of this marvelous machine.

It is as important for the teacher to keep up with what is going on in television as it is to keep up with the latest published materials. There are many programs which will be very valuable for language instruction and these should be assigned for home-viewing.

One very alert teacher of elementary French is making use of the interest her fourth, fifth, and sixth graders have in viewing a weekly series on television entitled "Combat." This deals with World War II and takes place in France. There are many scenes in small towns and villages where the natives speak in French. Although some of this speech is beyond the comprehension of these little students, many of the short sentences and exclamations are recognized by them with great excitement. It becomes a contest among them, the day after viewing, to see how much they recognized, understood, and are able to remember.

The interested, keen teacher will take advantage of every occasion which presents itself for using television to make the teaching and learning of the foreign language come alive. This should include in-school as well as home-viewing.

Programmed Instruction

One cannot leave the topic of new technology without giving some consideration to programmed instruction and its implications for foreign language teaching.

Programmed instruction is intended for self-instruction and is predicated on small-step emphasis. The student moves from step to step, giving his response at each step. If he is correct, the program is designed to corroborate the correctness of his answer. If he is wrong he cannot go ahead until he has produced the right answer.

The teaching machine is the name given to the instrument through which the program is sent. Teaching machines range in complexity from simple, manually operated devices to complicated, electrically driven ones. The simplest are boxes with slots through which the student sees first the question to which he responds and then the answer which he compares with his own response. In some of the very complicated teaching machines lights flash when the right answer is chosen and bells ring when the wrong one is offered.

The program need not necessarily be sent through a machine. It can be designed as a book with grids or shields which uncover the question and then the answer as the student progresses down the page. At each step he compares his answer to the one given and corrects his errors as he goes along.

There are several instructional programs in foreign languages for pronunciation, grammatical structures, and reading. Some are designed to be used with tape recorders and workbooks or manuals, others use printed materials only.

Programmed instruction has a very definite role to play in foreign language education. As with any other tool or instrument, programmed instruction can be as good or as bad as the material it contains.

Well-designed programs can be used with great profit for follow-up practice. The student proceeds at his own speed to practice the material which he has been taught. In the pre-reading period programmed instruction on sound tapes or records can relieve the teacher of the tedious task of administering drills and exercises. After the student has learned to read and write, the combination of tape recorder, in the language laboratory or out, with workbooks for the student can be invaluable for reinforcing sound with the sight of the printed word. This can help the student to develop his ability in the reading and writing phases of the study of the foreign language.

The author questions the efficacy of *self-instruction* on all levels in foreign language by programmed instruction. As stated many times, in the initial stages of the study of a foreign language, before the student has developed the ability to discriminate among the sounds of the foreign language, he is very dependent on the teacher's guidance, correction, and criticism. No instructional program can take the place of this responsibility of the teacher. At the more advanced levels where the student has a firm command of the sound and structure system of the language he might be able to cope with additional instruction by programming alone, without the teacher's guidance. However, for reinforcement and practice of material which has been taught by the teacher, programmed instruction can play a very effectual role in the follow-up procedures of foreign language development.

Can the foreign language teacher carry the whole foreign language instructional process on his shoulders armed with nothing more than his voice, the textbook, and a piece of chalk? Students perform best in the world they know best. Theirs is the age of technology and its marvels are almost commonplace to them. To reach the student of today, the teacher must bring some of that world into the classroom. Instruction becomes more interesting to the student as well as to the teacher.

More important, however, is the fact that the student becomes better equipped to perform in his electronic world if he is taught with electronic devices. For instance, he will be able to understand the foreign voice more easily when he hears it over a telephone, on the television or radio, or on films, if he is trained to understand the native voices on sound tape, film, or record in the classroom.

It is not unreasonable to assume that someday he may find himself in a situation where such performance would be required of him, be it for business or pleasure.

SUGGESTED READINGS:

Conwell, Marilyn, "An Evaluation of the Keating Report," *The Bulletin,* National Association of Secondary School Principals, Vol. 48, Washington, D.C., 1964.

Cross, A. J. Foy, and Cypher, Irene F., *Audio-Visual Education* (New York, Crowell, 1961).

Dale, Edgar, *Audio-Visual Methods in Teaching*, rev. ed. (New York, Holt, Rinehart and Winston, 1954).

Eaton, Esther, *et al.*, "Source Materials for Secondary School Teachers of Foreign Languages," Bulletin 1962 (OE-27001B), U.S. Department of Health, Education, and Welfare, Office of Education, Washington, D.C. 20202.

Hayes, Alfred S., *et al.*, "A New Look at Programmed Learning," Northeast Conference, 1962.

Hutchinson, J. S., "The Language Laboratory, Modern Foreign Languages in High School," Bulletin 1961 No. 23 (OE-27013), U.S. Department of Health, Education, and Welfare, Office of Education, Washington, D.C. 20202.

Johnston, Marjorie, C., *et al.*, "Foreign Language Laboratories in Schools and Colleges," Bulletin 1959 No. 3, U.S. Department of Health, Education, and Welfare, Washington, D.C. 20201.

Levenson, W. B., *et al.*, *Teaching Through Radio and Television* (New York, Holt, Rinehart and Winston, 1952).

Lumsdaine, A. A., *et al.*, "Teaching Machines and Programmed Learning," Department of Visual Instruction, National Education Association, Washington, D.C., 1960. 20036.

Ollman, Mary J., (ed.), MLA Selected List of Materials For Teachers of Modern Foreign Languages, Modern Language Association, 4 Washington Place, New York, N.Y. 10011.

Trow, William Clark, *Teacher and Technology—New Designs for Learning* (New York, Appleton-Century-Crofts, 1963).

FOR INFORMATION

Posters:

French: National Information Bureau—American Association of Teachers of French, 972 Fifth Ave., New York, N.Y. 10021.

Spanish: Spanish Cultural Services, Spanish Embassy, Washington, D.C.
Pan-American World Airways, 28-01 Bridge Plaza N., Long Island City, N.Y. 111.

German: German Consul General, 460 Park Ave., New York, N.Y. 10022.

Newspapers and Periodicals:

Etranger Hachette, 30 Madison Ave., New York, N.Y. 10017 (French).

European Media Representatives, Inc., 132 W. 43rd St., New York, N.Y. 10036 (French, Italian, Spanish, Polish).

Four Continent Book Corp., 156 Fifth Ave., New York, N.Y. 10010 (Russian).

German News Co., 200 E. 86th St., New York, N.Y. 10028 (German).

Instituto Italiano de Cultura, 686 Park Ave., New York, N.Y. 10021 (Italian).

Scholastic Magazines, 902 Sylvan Ave., Englewood Cliffs, N.J. 07632 (French, German, Russian, Spanish).

Programmed Instruction on French Pronunciation:

Teaching Audials and Visuals, Inc., 250 W. 57th St., New York, N.Y. 10019.

7
THE WRITTEN WORD—
READING AND WRITING

- Reading consists of many complicated mental processes.
- The student should progress from the simple act of reading aloud the lines he sees to the more complex activity of reading silently in order to comprehend and react to the thoughts implied beyond the printed word.
- The teacher by using effective techniques and materials will develop good and purposeful reading habits in the student.
- The student should learn to deduce meaning from the printed page by using various contextual devices.
- Capable students will benefit from reading material on all kinds of subject matter.
- There are many levels of the writing act which range from copying to writing creatively.
- For the most part the student will need to be guided in his writing activities by the teacher.
- The chalkboard can be the most effective tool which the teacher has for developing correct writing.

READING

What Is Reading?

Almost every language teacher could offer a different definition of this skill. His characterization would be colored by what he considers to be his aim in teaching the skill. Reading is not easily defined as one process which applies uniformly to all situations because it consists of a series of complex mental tasks. These tasks vary with the material which is being read and with the purpose for which it is being read. Comprehending the written word is a more involved process than would at first appear. It requires reliance on many different skills which must be identified by the teacher if they are to be developed in the student.

In the field of reading, the foreign language teacher would do well to look at what the reading specialists can tell him concerning this discipline. Ability to read and write have always been two of the aims of foreign language instruction. In the light of the new performance approach, however, re-examination of the role of reading is of great importance. Reading should not be taught in a vacuum. It should be a continuum of the oral and audio phases of the language and should be learned in conjunction with what the student understands and can say in the foreign language.

There are several dimensions to the reading act. Briefly, they can be identified as *reading the lines, reading between the lines* and *beyond the lines.* These steps represent the sequence to be achieved in foreign language instruction in reading. They represent the path along which the student must be led so as to develop the ability to read *directly* in the foreign language. To guide him to read *silently, independently,* and *intelligently* in order to interpret the meaning beyond the printed matter he sees is to help him achieve the highest level of the reading act. The eventual aim in all reading is silent, independent reading for information and pleasure.

Reading the Lines

Reading the lines implies not just seeing the letters of the word or phrase but recognizing the word because of some previous experience with it and consequently knowing its meaning.

We have already discussed the oral activity which is necessary before the student can be brought to the point where he can begin to read. (see page 32). Facility with language is one indication of readiness for reading. Control of the sound system of the language and a certain ability to handle a limited range of vocabulary and sentence structure are the minimum requirements.

Reading involves the ability to see the lines with the eye, to hear in the inner ear the differences between words which are very much alike and to be able to distinguish the specific differences. It involves, too, the understanding not only of the individual words but also the fusion of these which results in phrases or sentences. Word recognition is only part of the total process which results in comprehension.

Meaning can only be gleaned from phrases and related words and not from single words. This involves physical as well as mental effort since studies of how one reads reveals that the eye does not move from word to word but jumps from phrase to phrase. In the jumps the meaning of words in context is perceived.

Sentence or phrase sense is fundamental to reading comprehension. These become the keystones upon which meaning is built. Getting sense from reading a line of text depends on several items. We go from print to inner sound to meaning. Going from print to sound should be almost instantaneous. If this step is delayed it retards the reader's understanding. Intonation, and rhythm and melody of the language are fundamental to reading comprehension. Improper intonation distorts language and hampers comprehension, whereas good intonation combines melody and cadence so that phrases, clauses, and sentences are grouped significantly.

In the pre-reading period the student is involved in mimicking, reproducing, and comprehending the "phrase sense" of the material. In making the transition to reading every effort must be made to utilize all the student has learned about the oral aspect of the selection to insure the correctness of pronunciation, intonation, rhythm of phrases, and related structures and sentences. In the first contacts with the written language he should see only that which he can handle orally so that it does not degenerate into word-by-word reading.

Since the student has the sound of this material in his ear and understands what he is saying, what remains to be done is to show him the symbols which represent the sounds. Relating the sounds in the spoken words to the letters which represent them should be done with great care. If the student is presented with the printed script and no systematic effort is made to associate the phoneme (sounds) with the graphemes (letters), he will resort to applying those phonemes which he has been accustomed to associate with the graphemes in his native language. The careful preparation of the pre-reading period will then be negated and undone, and the student will have lost the benefit of that instruction.

The transition should be organized. Enough time should be taken by the teacher to insure successful achievement of this skill by every member of the class. There are several methods for bridging the gap between activity with the spoken language and activity with reading material. Some teachers use the word recognition system as a means for making the transition. In this method the printed version of a selection which he has studied orally is put in the hands of the student who follows the script silently while the teacher reads it aloud several times. Since it is familiar material the student associates the written form of the words with the sounds he has learned to pronounce. After the teacher has read the selection aloud several times, the class reads it first in full chorus, then in half a chorus. Finally individual students are called upon to read the whole passage or parts of it.

The teacher calls attention to unusual letter combinations, silent letters, and other items of which he thinks the student should be made aware. A sufficient number of readings is intended to give the student the insight into the relationship of the phonemes to the graphemes, through which he will acquire the recognition of the words of the selection. This should enable him to recognize these words whenever he meets them again and to recall their pronunciation. It is the author's opinion that, in foreign languages, the student needs more than word recognition to insure a smooth and lasting transition to the printed word. Instruction by phonics lays a better foundation upon which the student can rely for current as well as for all future associations of sound and symbols.

In the phonics method the teacher starts to bridge the gap several weeks before presenting the whole script to the student to read. Several phonemes and their corresponding graphemes are taught each day. These are taken from a sentence in a selection which the students have already learned to pronounce. A phoneme is selected and the teacher writes a one-syllable word on the board which contains that phoneme. For instance, he writes *bon* on the board as he pronounces the word. Under this he lists several more words which contain the sound and symbol, such as *ton*, and *mon*. He points out the letter combinations which produce the sound. He emphasizes the nasality produced by the final *n*. These, too, he pronounces as he writes them on the board. He may call on students to volunteer words which they have learned which appear to contain the same sound. These are listed in the same column if they belong there. After a sufficient number of examples have been contributed by teacher or students the class is asked to pronounce the whole list several times.

Then another phoneme taken from the same sentence is treated in the same way. This time words may be listed which contain both the phoneme which has already been learned and the new one if necessary. When all the phonemes which need attention have been thoroughly drilled so that the sound of the words has been associated with the sight of the printed form, the teacher writes on the board the sentence from which the phonemes were selected. These are read several times by teacher and student, making sure that the original pronunciation, intonation, and rhythm are preserved. This will be the first time that the student sees the printed forms of the phrase groupings in this sentence. Emphasis should be placed on the fact that the individual words blend into phrases and are meaningful in context only. At the second reading the teacher should signal silent letters and other extraordinary items of written language such as incidents of linking and elision, which were not mentioned before.

The teacher continues this procedure until all the graphemes of the language have been taught to the students, several at a time, all based on sentences which have previously been learned orally. The complexity of the written system of the language will determine how long the teacher will spend on this transition. Those languages such as Russian, Chinese or Hebrew, whose alphabet does not resemble the alphabet of the English language will require more time to learn how to form the letters than those languages like French or Spanish whose alphabets use essentially the same letters as we do in English. In the latter languages, however, more time will be required to insure that the student does not carry over into the foreign language the sound values which he has been in the habit of associating with the letters in his native language.

The more care with which one bridges the gap between sound and the printed word, the better will be the lasting rewards. When the student has comprehended the written system of the language, he is ready for the first level of reading—that of reading the lines.

Reading the lines or achieving literal comprehension is the skill of getting direct meaning from phrases or sentences in context. For this first contact we should give the student a script for which he can give a good oral reading, and whose meaning is clear to him. This serves a two-fold purpose.

Preparing the student for good silent reading in the future is the first reason for choosing already learned oral material. One cannot begin too soon to avoid poor silent reading where sentences are broken up into word-by-word reading or meaningless fragments from which no comprehension or, at best, poor comprehension, results. A selection which has been properly learned orally, begins to establish good silent reading habits where correct intonation is preserved and where structural patterns and parts of sentences are joined by proper function words and where the reader has an overall feeling of the sentence sense of the foreign language.

Secondly, in order to teach the student to read the lines well it is important that he understand what he is reading. There are several procedures which the teacher can use to ascertain if the student has read well. Each of these requires answers to questions which are to be found in the text itself. Direct questions, true-false exercises, and multiple choice sentences may be used for checking understanding. This is the initial stage of the reading process on the lowest level, because it requires little or no interpretation on the part of the student. It does, however, require careful reading of the lines to find the answers.

READING BETWEEN AND BEYOND THE LINES

In pursuit of the goal of independent, silent, intelligent reading for information and pleasure, the teacher should carry literal comprehension—reading the lines—on to the next step, that of reading between and beyond the lines. This involves reflecting on what the author has said and reacting to it, and is more difficult than merely perceiving phrases or sentences. The reader is required to think about what he is reading and to supply many meanings which are not stated but which are implied in the words of the text.

Interpretation of textual content makes the reader a student of what he is reading and not a slave to recitation. Learning to read between the lines is a skill which must be developed carefully in the student. He needs to be led and guided by the teacher to acquire the necessary habits, skills, and insight. Interpretation and evaluation are more difficult to teach and are frequently overlooked by many teachers who do not go beyond the literal reading of a text.

The teacher who gives instruction in reading is like the juggler in the three-ring circus who is trying to keep several balls in the air at the same time.

- He must not lose sight of the audio and lingual activities of the students for it is upon these that the development of the reading skills depends.
- He must develop the students' ability to read by strengthening their knowledge of the structure of the language.
- He must aid their comprehension by giving them insight into how to increase their vocabularies.
- He must reinforce their literal understanding of the language.
- He must guide them into interpreting and evaluating what might lie between and beyond the words that the author has written.

Teaching students to read is a problem which confronts almost every teacher on every level of instruction, in English as well as in foreign languages. Our students are not always drawn to reading since they can get information and entertainment by means of other media. The student has many blocks to overcome before he can be expected voluntarily to pick up reading matter in the foreign language. We cannot teach him how to read if he does not want to read.

However, some subject exists which interests each one of us. The trick is to find that subject. Even the most lackadaisical student will respond if the teacher can find what really appeals to him and can draw upon his interest. What a person gets out of reading a text is determined by his background, his experiences, and by what he brings to the material to be read. The degree of reflection or concentration is determined by the reader's purpose or his reason for wanting to understand the passage. It may also depend upon how much knowledge he brings to the ideas presented to him by the author. The slowest reader will make the effort to read something if it will give him information he desires to have.

With all of this in mind, the teacher needs two kinds of reading tools for every class—classroom material for instruction and demonstration of methods, devices, and techniques; and materials for independent reading to which the student will go to find something which interests him, and which he wants to read. To the material he has chosen he will apply what he has been taught in class. The materials are self-selected, but what he is required to do with them will be assigned by the teacher. The classroom material which is used can be selections in a supplementary reader or even in the textbook if they are interesting enough.

Most teachers find that short selections or short stories are more interesting to the students than a long story which drags out over an extended period of time. The advantage of reading from a collection of short stories is that the student encounters many different kinds of situations, plots, and characters. He is exposed to the writing style of several different authors. A short story also gives the student the chance to see a plot begun, developed, and concluded in a short space of time. For all of these reasons, a book of short stories makes a good classroom reader.

Whatever is chosen will serve the teacher as a vehicle

through which to teach and demonstrate all the necessary devices for interpreting and evaluating a reading text. The work with the classroom materials must be of the highest quality. The aim is not to "cover" as many pages of the text as possible but to illustrate through this reading matter the various methods and procedures which the teacher chooses to develop.

Every new selection for study in the classroom must be read aloud first by the teacher. Since most reading matter is written with a developmental plan in mind and is intended to be read from beginning to end without interruption, it should be presented to the student that way for the first time. If it is too long for a reading at one sitting it should be divided into parts which have logical breaks so that the student's interest will be sustained until he gets to the next part. The student should be made to listen to the first reading of the text with books closed so that he will have the sound of the language in his ear before he reads it.

Listening, with the book closed, forces the student to give his undivided attention to the presentation in order to get meaning from the words. A good oral rendition gives the student the chance to hear the groupings of phrases and clauses through which the sense of the sentence emerges. This oral reading should give him the pleasure of an uninterrupted listening experience whereby he may gain meaning from the language he already knows, as well as spontaneous meaning and pleasure from context, gestures, and inferences. The first reading should be accompanied by visuals and other devices which will help the student to derive meaning from the spoken language.

The second reading should again be done by the teacher. This time the students should have their books open before them. With the book open the student should be able to match the written words to the sounds he is hearing. During the second reading the teacher should further clarify by pointing, gestures, or visuals, the meaning of those words which are absolutely essential to the meaning of the selection. Vocabulary building (see page 109) will take place at another time when it does not interfere with the pleasure of reading the selection as a whole. The student should be encouraged to guess at the meaning of unknown words by their context or appearance (see page 108). Several more oral readings by full chorus, half chorus, and finally by some individuals should follow. Students should never be permitted to read aloud until they have heard several model readings by the teacher.

A few questions on the literal comprehension will give the teacher an idea of how much the student has understood and how much more explanation is needed at this point. When he is satisfied that the meaning of the selection is understood, he should introduce some device which will make the student rearrange, consider, or search for the ideas which the author has expressed. He should introduce one such technique at a time and go into the procedure slowly, making sure that every student understands what he is doing. It would be wise to start with the simplest device and progress to the more difficult ones. Some devices or techniques may require more practice time than others. The teacher may want to come back to one or more of them several times. In these procedures he should be striving to make the student think, reflect, and react to what he is reading.

The following are some of the techniques a teacher can use to stimulate the student to think about what he is reading.

- Select the cue words or phrases in the paragraph (or on the page) upon which the meaning of the selection depends.
- Join the cue words or phrases together in such a way that a summary results. (The teacher will have to teach such summarizing expressions as: as a result of, for these reasons, in conclusion, because of, in order that, however, in spite of, that is to say, etc.)
- Make an outline showing main ideas and the contributing ones.
- Find the items in the selection with which you agree.
- Find the items in the selection with which you disagree. Can you give reasons?
- Could you give the selection another title? What would you choose and why?
- Can you give this story a different ending?
- What generalizations can you make after reading the selection?

- If you were turning this story into a play what would you need on the stage? Find the items in the story.
- Retell the story in your own words.

These are only suggestions. The ingenious teacher will find many more ideas for getting the student to think about what he has read. The teacher should treat only one of these techniques at a time when dealing with classroom reading material. The student should be encouraged to express his ideas. This kind of activity should help to develop positive habits and attitudes toward reading.

Although the preparation and training for good reading habits may be done with a group, reading itself finally becomes individual and personal. The student will eventually be reading by himself, alone and unsupervised. If he has been properly guided he will thereafter be able to interpret intelligently and make good judgments unaided. In preparation for such personal profitable reading the teacher must have supplementary reading matter along with the basic classroom material which is read by the class.

For this the teacher should have a classroom collection of all kinds of reading material. A set of bookshelves in the classroom can serve to house the printed matter from which the student can choose what he wants to read. The material should be diversified and, in order for everyone to be able to begin, should contain easy, short selections. These items should cover a wide range of topics so that the student can choose the one which is of interest to him. Magazine advertisements, newspaper announcements, or even the written matter on cereal or soap powder boxes can make good "starters" for some. The collection should also contain novelettes, short stories, and duplicated articles to which the student can progress. Materials with illustrations are particularly good since the pictures help the student to understand the text. Popular magazine stories are usually desirable because they are dramatic and exciting.

The length and the content of the selection which the student chooses should not matter at all. Even such items as recipes, or advertisements could be acceptable at the beginning of this period of independent reading. If the student finds his own material so much the better. The only requirement should be that it must be entirely in the foreign language. The quality and scope of the independent reading should improve as the student goes along.

This material is for reading at home and for practicing the skills which have been taught in class. If the lesson has been devoted to learning how to summarize, the student will be required to summarize the selection he has chosen to read at home. If the lesson in class has been devoted to learning how to generalize, the homework assignment will require the student to do the same thing with his reading matter at home. The homework assignments will then be read or discussed in class.

The outside, independent reading should continue to gain in importance as the term advances. A record should be kept for each student noting the type and length of the selections read. Special rewards should be offered to the underachiever as well as to the bright student. Recognition can be given for increasing the length, the number, and the variety of the selections read. Such rewards could serve as incentives to encourage everyone to try longer and longer reading material and to read widely on many different kinds of topics. The teacher must be always on the alert, however, to prevent rapid reading from becoming careless reading.

It is very important to provide the opportunity for sharing the results of self-directed reading with the class. Toward the middle of the term every student should decide on an end-of-term culminating project. The project could take such forms as an illustrated talk, a demonstration of some kind, or an oral report. It should require several weeks to prepare during which the student will need to read in many different sources. The topic and the project should be confirmed and discussed in short, individual conferences with the teacher. The student will thus be guided in his reading and preparation for his performance. These projects often turn out to be the most exciting activity of the entire school year for the student.

This kind of individual endeavor allows the bright student to find his level of achievement and it also provides the opportunity for the underachiever to become involved in performing with something which is within his capacity and which is of intrinsic interest to him. In this way the teacher also takes advantage of the individual tastes, interests, and talents of his students and puts them to use to develop reflective thinking or "reading beyond the lines." An annotated bibliography should be submitted by the student when the project is completed.

How can the teacher expect the student to read new material, at home, the vocabulary and structures of which may be unfamiliar to him? Reading is not a matter of knowing the meaning of every word in every sentence. Reading involves "reaching" for the meaning of the "unknowns" through the clues which appear on the page and the background which the reader brings to the passage. The desire to reach lies in the reader's interest and his purpose for achieving understanding.

Equally important, however, is the teacher's attitude toward inferences. The student will attempt to reach for comprehension if he knows that he will not be punished for making incorrect deductions. With encouragement, guidance, and proper preparation he will learn how to reach and make valid inferences.

REACHING IN READING

Along with classroom instruction in reading and supervising the independent reading of the students, the teacher should also teach in depth techniques for building vocabulary and for reinforcing language usage. These activities should never be allowed to break into a reading unit. They may be covered in several consecutive periods after a reading selection has been completed.

Before the student was brought to the point of reading the printed word, the teacher was primarily involved in teaching him to manipulate and use the structures he was being taught. This was done with a very limited vocabulary so that the student would not be confronted by the double handicap of learning new vocabulary and new structure at the same time.

However, when the student starts to learn to read he should begin to systematically build up his vocabulary and his language sense. The incentive for wanting to learn these skills should come directly out of the student's independent reading material. He should be encouraged to use all the techniques which are discussed below. Where he cannot divine the meaning of a passage because he is unable to understand key phrases, he should bring his problem to class along with his homework. The teacher should organize these phrases and build around them the vocabulary study of the class. In this way teacher and students are providing information which is needed by all the members of the class, thereby, motivating the lesson.

Every one of us has a vocabulary of various shades. There are words and expressions which we know very well and use frequently and correctly. There are others we do not know quite so well, although we recognize them and know them when we meet them. There are still other expressions we know vaguely; we are not quite sure of their exact meaning. Finally, there are those we do not know at all. These latter we need to guess at through contextual clues if we desire to understand the passage in which they appear.

All of us learn new words frequently and rarely do we need to use the dictionary to discover their meaning. Those expressions which we know vaguely today may suddenly become part of our active vocabulary if we meet them often enough and if we need to use them. Those which we do not know at all and whose meaning we infer today may also move up in the scale of recognition and become better known to us if we meet them several times in different contexts.

We are constantly reaching for meaning in the spoken as well as the written language. We grasp the general meaning of a statement by making use of what we know about language and what we know about people and things. We must encourage our students to do this when they are reading at home.

Every language has unmistakable features. You do not have to know much about a language to recognize it by its special characteristics. The nouns look different from the verbs, the adjectives are rarely mistaken for prepositions. The past tenses look different from the future and the present tenses. Plurals can be distinguished from singulars. These things we learn about a language very early in our experience with it. We can therefore make some educated guesses about the syntax of words and we can "reach" for meaning with a fair degree of certainty. The meaning we reach for in one sentence or paragraph may be corroborated or corrected by our next encounter with it in another sentence. It will enter into our active vocabulary if we meet it often enough but will remain passive if we do not use it.

We can guess the meaning of words *by the context* in which we find them. What precedes or follows may give us a clue to their meaning. For example we can guess the meaning of X by its use in the following sentence. "A big, black, cackling X circled around my head and almost brushed against my hair with its outspread wings." We can certainly guess that X is a big, black bird. There are several clues in the sentence which lead us to guess that the X is a bird, even though the exact name of the bird may be unfamiliar to us.

We can also guess the season by the context of sentences. For instance, "It was in the X that I met him, at that time of year when the daffodils were all in bloom." From what we know about the time of year when daffodils bloom we can guess the season which is indicated in the sentence. We can also guess the place by the same process. In the sentence, "The X was beautiful to see with the blue waves rolling gently on the white sand," there is no doubt that X must refer to some kind of beach.

Words themselves often offer us clues to their meaning. Words which contain the same stem may look alike except for their endings. Sometimes a closer examination of a word which at first glance looked unfamiliar reveals something recognizable. Subtracting the noun endings, verb endings, or participial endings often discloses a root of a known word. This is also true of prefixes and suffixes.

The study of antonyms and paraphrases will be of considerable help to the student in building up his vocabulary. It is a good idea to have each student keep a notebook with a list of the newly learned words with their paraphrased meanings. Requiring them to write a sentence first with the new word and then with its paraphrase will help to fix in the minds of the students the meaning of the newly acquired expressions.

The study of idiomatic expressions will find its way into the language lessons, too, by way of the word lists of the students. They will often turn out to be the key phrases which are not understandable. Enough practice will help the student to recognize them as idiomatic expressions even if they do not understand them.

Cognates should be handled with care. There are good ones and bad ones. The look-alike words may be grossly misleading for they frequently do not carry the same meaning in both languages. For example, the man who is *blessé* is anything but blessed. The word *coin* in French has nothing to do with numismatics nor does the word *wand* in German have anything to do with fairies.

However, sound sometimes helps us to identify a word which looks very different because of the way it is spelled. When it is pronounced, however, the sound of the word becomes familiar. For instance *donjon* does not look much like *dungeon,* but when it is sounded one could easily guess at its meaning in context.

Synonyms, too, must be studied with great care since two words which appear to have similar meanings may actually mean very different things. It is almost always better to use paraphrases than synonyms.

The dictionary should be used very rarely. When it is used it should not be an English-to-foreign-language book but a dictionary in which the words and their meanings are given in the foreign language. Dictionary work should be done in class along with the other vocabulary building exercises.

As the techniques, which have been discussed above, are being taught, the student should be given enough drill and repetition so that he becomes familiar with each one. Through their use he should begin to learn to read with facility. This skill should become stronger as he does more reading. In the last analysis, the value of the techniques which are taught is dependent upon the worth which the student attaches to the reading process.

It is our purpose not only to guide and teach him, but to give him the opportunities for discovering how pleasurable and meaningful reading can be. Our students will never disappoint us if we do not stifle them and if we show them that we do not underestimate their intelligence.

READING AND LITERATURE

If the acquisition and utilization of foreign language skills are to be of continuing importance to the greatest number of students, the study of the classics in literature must not be the only goal toward which all their efforts are directed. We are all aware, even if we do not admit it to ourselves, that a sharp decline in interest occurs in most students when they are presented with the seemingly endless task of unravelling the intricacies of a piece of literature which we have decided is "good for them to read."

If it is our fond hope that by making them read "good literature" they will be converted to that activity and will seek more of it on their own, we have not really taken a good look at our students since they left our schools and classrooms. The great majority of them undoubtedly have avoided picking up a book to read which was written by one of the authors whose works they were forced to study in their literature lessons in class.

The study of literary landmarks has its place in the continuum of foreign language instruction. However, it is an activity which requires a very thorough knowledge of the foreign language. One cannot expect a student with an inadequate command of the language to appreciate the style of the literary giants. He is not expected to read the classics in his own language until he has had many years of experience with reading. It is not realistic to think that a student who has spent only one or two academic years studying it will have acquired sufficient feeling to appreciate the beauty, the subtleties of the literary quality of the foreign language, the nuances of the author's thought.

An advanced student of a foreign language, however, *should* learn to appreciate its literary masterpieces for their esthetic value. An intelligent student should be trained through a few literature courses in the techniques of close reading. In the hands of a competent teacher he should acquire a sensitivity to the written language and learn to recognize its nuances as presented by adroit authors. He should be guided to the approaches and methods which he can apply to his own future reading of literary works in the foreign language if and when he has the desire to do such reading.

However, literary writings should not be the only reading matter to which the student is asked to apply the skill he has acquired. Literature should take its place and proper relationship to those other materials to which a capable, intelligent student may be expected to give his time and attention.

Courses of study for the advanced student should be designed to include other kinds of reading matter. In such a curriculum, the writings which reveal the social and historical background of an era might well be included together with those which deal with its art, music, and literature. For instance, instead of Literature of the 19th Century, the course could be entitled The 19th Century in France (or Spain, etc.) and could deal with those writings which reveal the causes and effects of the events in all areas which distinguish that century from the ones which preceded and the ones which followed.

Such correlated reading could be initiated in the advanced courses in the high school. On the college level similar integrated courses could be given with more emphasis on reading in the original works. The able student would thus strengthen his ability to read critically and to intelligently analyze what he has read. Properly motivated, he might seek writings of all kinds and might read widely on many subjects. He might find a field of interest either in the arts or in sociology which he might wish to explore in depth. If he has been given the training and he has acquired the necessary skills, he will be able to read material on any topic with insight and intelligence.

WRITING

Being able to express one's thoughts in writing directly in the foreign language without resorting to the use of English is the goal toward which one aspect of foreign language instruction should be directed. In writing as in reading, the teacher is concerned with several different levels and dimensions of the writing act. His first concern should be to have the student make every effort to perfect the form of the words and lines which he sets down on paper. He must be able to spell correctly, and to write the sentences without errors in structure and syntax.

On the next level of writing, the teacher should be concerned with training the student to manipulate the structures so that they convey the ideas he is seeking to express. Learning to use structures and to write them correctly should engage the student's and the teacher's efforts throughout the entire study of the language.

On the highest level is the student who is writing creatively. The teacher should be concerned with guiding the student who possesses this special talent in his choice of expressions, imagery, and in the fine points of his writing style.

The writing skill should be developed along with the reading skill since each of these graphic skills reinforces the other. Writing depends on subliminal pronunciation as much as reading does (see page 97). It is therefore essential to start by teaching the student to write what he knows how to read and pronounce.

COPYING

The first step in learning to write is to copy exactly from a good model. Such activity should begin the day the student begins to bridge the gap between the sound and the printed word (see page 98). As the lists of graphemes are being developed, the student should begin to write them in his notebook. He is not only learning to recognize the symbols which represent the sounds he has been pronouncing, but is also reinforcing this study by learning to write them. His homework assignments should require him to copy these lists several times. In this way he is reviewing his pronunciation as well as his reading and relating them both to his writing.

Along with single words, the student should be required to include in his copying activities sentences and short paragraphs. These items must come out of the selections which the student already knows how to read correctly. He should be required to copy this material several times for homework assignments.

Short, daily dictation practice (see page 118) will be used to determine how well the student has learned to write the material he has copied.

Another form of copying requires the student to answer questions based on a reading selection. Although this, too, is exact duplication, it does require a little more thinking on the part of the student because he must select the right answer out of the text.

Exact copying focuses the student's attention on such matters as accents, silent letters, verb endings, and other elements special to the written form of the language. Dictation exercises help to reinforce his recognition of these phenomena and fix them in his memory. Even as the student advances in the acquisition of the skill of independent writing, occasional copying exercises can prove very useful.

DIRECTED WRITING

Since good writing depends on the recognition of sentence construction the next step in the development of the writing skill should concern itself with sentence structure. At first this should be done by presenting the student with a minimum of difficulties. To ask him to compose whole sentences requires him to solve too many problems at one time—problems of vocabulary, structure, spelling. To insure good writing in the future he must be confronted with one problem at a time until he develops the competency to write whole sentences correctly.

Exercises where the student is required *to complete segments* of a sentence guide him in the acquisition of sentence sense yet require him to concentrate on only one thing at a time. These drills may ask him to complete a sentence by choosing the proper word or phrase from a list. Or he may be required, by some clue in the sentence, to use a part of speech or a tense of a verb which he has already studied.

Scrambled sentences oblige the student to rearrange the words into well-constructed sentences and are very good exercises for developing structure and syntax sense. The student who is just beginning to write is provided with all the ingredients for writing a correct sentence, something which he could not do on his own at this point.

Requiring the student to *make minimal changes* such as changing nouns to pronouns or singulars to plurals develops in him an awareness of syntactical relationships. These are highlighted because only the structures under study are manipulated. The rest of the sentence is provided and need not be composed by the student. Such exercises as changing direct discourse to indirect discourse or recasting a passage from one person to another or from one tense to another also require manipulation on the part of the student without presenting him with the many problems of writing the whole passage himself.

Another writing exercise could require the student to compose a telegram or cable which is based on a selection which he is given to read. Here the student is trained to pick out the basic important ideas and arrange them so that the message is delivered. An exercise in the reverse process can also be used. The student is given a cable or telegram and is asked to expand the text by providing details which the shorter message did not give.

Gradually the teacher can guide the student to approach an individual writing style and can still exert the kind of control which keeps the student thinking in the foreign language as well as writing in it. Cued narrations are of value since they give him a beginning sentence and a list of cue words and phrases. He uses these hints and constructs a short passage around them. For example:

> Mary loves to sing.   to get together   guitar
>   friends   to enjoy oneself

Almost every student will write a different selection to express his own ideas. Cued narratives can grow in size and difficulty as the students learn to handle the language.

Passages which supply only basic sentences can become descriptive narratives when the students supply adjectives for them. The students may be required to use one or two adjectives with each noun. At first these adjectives may be presented by the teacher in a list from which the student chooses. Later on they may be made to come from the student's own active vocabulary.

Another device for helping the student develop a writing style is to require him to retell a passage changing direct discourse to indirect discourse or vice versa. The direct discourse could take the form of a short playlet in which a description of stage setting is necessary and where the incidental actions of the actors on the stage need to be indicated.

Retelling stories so that they take place at seasons of the year or times of day or at locations which are different from those which occur in the original story is another scheme for writing within a given framework. The student is given a certain degree of freedom in his writing but is kept thinking in the foreign language. It is important to devise such schemes which will give the student enough help so that he will not need to resort to first composing his material in English before writing it in the foreign language.

Letters of invitation, applications for positions, telegrams, or thank you notes can be initiated by the teacher and sufficiently cued so that the student can produce well-written material. The teacher will thus be given the opportunity to show the students the authentic salutations and endings for this kind of writing.

The independent reading which the student has been doing should suggest to the teacher many writing projects. Starting with summaries of what has been read in newspapers and periodicals and advertisements and having acquired the necessary vocabulary, the student can go on to converting these resumés into other kinds of writing forms. The sports fans might want to write out interviews or questionnaires to present to those members of the class who are on the various school teams. The amateur journalist might be interested in preparing a news report or a weather report for use on radio or TV. Other journalistic projects might include writing a short article with headlines and sub-headlines on a current school event for an imaginary newspaper.

The girls might be interested in writing short articles about the newest trends in the fashion or culinary world. Readings on the woman's page of newspapers and magazines might result in reports of interesting things dealing with the house or the household.

With enough practice in this kind of semi-directed writing

the student will eventually be able to express himself without the help of cues or hints or other aids. These efforts could be directed to the production of a one or two page classroom newspaper.

The occasional issuance of such a newspaper can provide the necessary impetus for the creative writer by giving him the opportunity for release. The few individuals who are gifted and who write imaginatively need individual attention and guidance from the teacher. Writing for a class newspaper gives the student and his teacher a better opportunity for contact than does a classroom situation. Providing the vehicle for publication of his efforts will go a long way toward inspiring the creative writer to develop and test his skills.

THE DICTATION EXERCISE

Dictation is an activity which obliges the student to write the language which he hears spoken either by the teacher or by a tape or a record. The ability to promptly and correctly write the words and phrases which are being spoken in the foreign language requires considerable ability and knowledge in several areas.

- It requires the ability to discriminate between the sounds of the language.
- It requires the ability to transpose quickly the sounds of the language into the written symbols.
- It requires of the writer a knowledge of the grammatical structure of the language so that he can write correct sentences.
- It requires the writer to possess enough knowledge to be able to choose correctly from several homonyms so that he can write sensible sentences.

For all these reasons the student's introduction to the process of taking dictation should be made by easy steps. When he is beginning to learn to write in the foreign language dictation exercises should be based on previously studied material. No one should be expected to write correctly language which he does not understand. The first exercises of dictation will be given to verify the correct spelling of words or phrases from material which was used for copying. This is done in little exercises which are called spot dictations. In a spot dictation the student is given a written selection in which there are several blank spaces. The teacher reads the selection and the student is required to complete the sentences by inserting the missing words in the blanks as he hears them pronounced. At the beginning the spot dictations may leave out only a few words here and there. As the student becomes more adept at writing, the blank spaces should become larger and more frequent. When he has developed all the necessary skills, he should be able to take the whole dictation exercise directly and entirely from the spoken language.

There is an accepted procedure for giving dictation exercises which has proven to be very efficient because it gives the student at least three opportunities to hear the whole selection. The selection is first read through from the beginning to the end at normal speed. This initial reading gives the student the chance to concentrate on the language he hears and to prepare himself mentally for writing. It is a good idea to require that all pens and pencils be placed on the desk so that no one is tempted to write during the first reading.

The students are then asked to take their pens or pencils and write while the selection is being read for the second time. The selection is read in meaningful phrases with sufficiently long pauses in which the student can write what he hears. All punctuation marks and paragraph indications are given during this reading. It is very important that the pauses be timed so that they are neither too long nor too short. Too long a pause permits the student to dawdle and to lose his train of thought; too short a pause causes him to hurry and does not give him the time to think about what he is writing.

The third reading is a recapitulation of the selection including all the punctuation marks and paragraph signals. This reading is presented at normal speed and the selection is read through from beginning to end without pauses. During the third reading the student is given the opportunity to look over his work and make whatever changes are necessary.

In order to provide a model against which the class can check its work, it is a good idea to send a good student to a blackboard which is out of the line of vision of the class. He writes his dictation on the board while the rest of the class is writing at their seats. After the third reading the dictation on the board is corrected by the teacher. Only then is this board displayed to the class. The members of the class either correct their own or each other's papers using the dictation on the board as their model.

Dictation exercises need not be long to be effective educational tools. They should be used frequently to recapitulate what has been taught. Although they appear to be exercises of writing, they are in reality exercises which involve many skills.

WRITING ON THE CHALKBOARD

A good part of the student's writing activities are concerned with his daily homework assignments. It is through these exercises that he is required to write to reinforce what he has been taught in the classroom. However, since this writing is done by the student without an authoritative source to observe and correct him, homework which he brings to class is liable to contain errors.

Although the writing of the homework assignment is an individual activity, the correction of the assignment should benefit the whole class. It should serve the teacher as a device for further teaching and the student as a device for further learning.

We know that what we see can make a lasting impression and will probably be remembered for a long time. It is from this point of view that we must consider the correction of the homework assignment as well as everything else which is written on the board.

In view of the fact that what is written on the board is likely to be in the eye of the student, to be scrutinized by him and his classmates many, many times during the class period, it is good pedagogy to have only correct, clearly-written work on the board for them to see, to be impressed by, and to remember. Nothing incorrect should ever be written on the board by student or teacher. Students who are sent to the board rarely write their portion of the assignment without errors. Then, too, most students do not know how to write legibly on the board. It is therefore better not to send students to the board to write. There are other, more efficient techniques for the correction of the homework assignment.

An exercise which was given as homework and which needs correction should provide oral as well as written practice. The teacher should begin the correction of the assignment by having a student read a part of the exercise aloud. Immediate correction can be made orally by the students in the class or by the teacher. The correct sentence should then be repeated by the whole class once or twice. In this way every student participates in the correction of the entire exercise and not only in that part which is assigned to him to be written on the board. Everyone in the class hears and pronounces each correct sentence before it is written on the board for all to see.

The sentence should then be written on the board by the teacher. Each sentence of the assignment is corrected orally first, and repeated by the class before it is written on the board by the teacher. A reliable student who writes legibly and who can be depended on to write correctly can relieve the teacher of this task from time to time. This privilege is bestowed only on a student who performs well.

Managing board work in this manner offers several advantages.

- Homework correction is fast.
- Errors are corrected immediately.
- Students are never asked to write or to read incorrect material.
- Sentences are written in the correct order and placed so that they can be seen by everyone.
- It gives the entire class an active part in the correction of the exercise as well as the opportunity to hear and speak the language.
- It insures correct work which if left on the board will provide the class with model sentences and perfect forms and structures to look at.

- Oral correction by numerous members of the class can provide the astute teacher with an immediate check of those
students who have done their assignments and those who
have not.
- Yesterday's absentee benefits from the assignment he missed
by joining in the choral repetitions with the rest of the class
and by copying the sentences as they are written on the
board.

Other forms of work which appear on the board are those
which are written by the teacher in conjunction with the teaching of a lesson. Everything which the teacher needs to write on
the board for purposes of presenting a lesson should be planned
in advance. It should be included in the lesson plan. Words scrib-
bled helter-skelter all over the board wherever the teacher hap-
pens to be standing are not likely to be effective for teaching or
for learning. The boardwork should implement the teaching of
the lesson and when completed should reflect its design and purpose.

That which is written on the board should be so organized
that it synthesizes the lesson for the student and leaves a lasting
impression on him of what has been taught. The arrangement
should be so clear that the student can copy it into his notebook
for future reference, if necessary. Colored chalk used for headings or emphasis will enhance the board and will help instruction
immeasurably.

It is a good idea for the teacher to make an outline or plan
of what is to be written on the board on a small index card. This
card should be kept on the chalk rail where it will be handy for
reference. An isolated word, written on the board for a reason
unrelated to the plan should be written clearly on a board away
from the plan of the lesson. After it has served its purpose it
should be erased. This will do away with all the clutter which
accumulates on a board and which becomes confusing and meaningless as the period progresses.

After writing, the teacher should stand a little away from
the board to read what has been written. It is not easy to see errors in spelling when one stands too close. A little distance be-

tween the teacher and the board will make for easier reading and quicker detection of mistakes.

The handwriting on the board should be large and bold. It is a good idea to walk to the rear of the room to view from there what has been written. If it has been written clearly enough it should be easily read from that distance.

SUGGESTED READINGS:

Northeast Conference on the Teaching of Foreign Languages, "Reading for Meaning," Reports of the Working Committees, 1963.

Northeast Conference on the Teaching of Foreign Languages, "Writing as Expression," Reports of the Working Committees, 1963.

Seibert, Louise C., and Crocker, L. D., *Skills and Techniques for Reading French* (Baltimore, Johns Hopkins, 1960).

Twaddell, Freeman, *Foreign Language Instruction at the Second Level* (New York, Holt, Rinehart and Winston, 1963).

For information on foreign language newspapers and periodicals see page 94.

8

THE APPROACH TO
A CULTURE AND
A FOREIGN LANGUAGE

- The culture of a people influences every aspect of the life of every man in that society including his language.
- The instructor must teach a language by relating it to the culture to which it belongs. Ingenuity and a knowledge of sociology will help the teacher in this task.
- The student should participate in many culturally oriented activities.
- The language club can contribute greatly to giving the student cultural insight into the language he is studying.
- Cultural "spectaculars" can be used to focus the attention of the community on the importance of foreign language instruction.

WHAT IS THE CULTURE OF A PEOPLE?

The culture of a people is the total way of life shared by those who live in the same society. The culture of a people pervades every aspect of life in that society controlling its lives and tongues. It determines the form of the individual's behavior and language. It consists of apparent things such as actions, reactions, gestures, manners of greeting, houses, modes of transportation, food, as well as those intangible aspects of a society such as attitudes, philosophy, and beliefs. It shapes men physically, intellectually, emotionally, and morally and sets a limit to what a man can do and say, what he eats and when, what he sits and sleeps on, how and where he shows his emotions, what he can say and how he says it, and what he believes in. Every experience of a man's life is a reflection of what he has acquired from his culture.

Every culture is the product of a long and complex history. The culture of a people is transmitted by teaching of some sort, from one generation to the next. Cultural behavior, the customs and traditions, is shared by the whole population of a society. A culture depends on people for perpetuation, yet it outlives all of them.

Every culture contains an infinite number of behavior patterns. These patterns are interrelated and to some degree reinforce each other. A culture maintains itself when its members think, feel, and act alike in many situations. This culturally required behavior satisfies personal needs.

A culture of a people is both changing and unchanging. It is in constant transition, yet basically stable. It is the total of the established values of a society as well as the newest innovations which are continuously invading it.

THE CULTURAL APPROACH AND THE TEACHER

How can the teacher begin to approach this vast topic which is so intangible that it defies neat, compact definition and yet is so pervasive that it must permeate every aspect of foreign language instruction? How does a teacher give the student who is the product of one culture a "feeling" for people of another culture?

By its very nature, culture confounds anyone who tries to organize and systematize it. It does not fit into neat, little pigeonholes. It goes beyond well-ordered lesson plans. We have said that culture is constant yet always changing, that ideologies may appear to be permanent but that changing circumstances render values temporary. Which of these should the foreign language teacher be most concerned with, the permanent or the temporary? When and how should he bring this into his teaching? How much time should he devote to culture in foreign language instruction?

Does the teacher who shows slides of cathedrals and plays

records of folk songs give his students a feeling for other people? Does he bring insight into the Mexican's way of life when he shows his students a *piñata* or a *rebozo*? Does he thus give the student enough food for reflective thought? Can they learn to discover and appraise through these objects the cultural values of another people?

Presenting culture is very much like making a patch-work quilt. Each patch is made separately. Its design may be interesting enough to examine and enjoy for itself, but patches remain patches until they are attached to a permanent base in which their designs and shapes blend and relate to one another to make a recognizable whole.

Bits and pieces of information, interesting anecdotes, objects like the *piñata* and the *rebozo*, pictures, songs, and dances which the teacher brings to the attention of the class are interesting in themselves and merit attention and examination. But they remain bits and pieces until the teacher can skillfully relate and attach them to the larger design, the culture, the civilization to which they belong. Partial, isolated cultural impressions can result in misinterpretations, stereotypes of social patterns, and excessive sentimentality. Excessive infatuation and exaggerated opinions on the part of the teacher distorts the culture he is presenting. The student may be very disappointed when he meets the "real thing."

Acquainting the student with the culture of foreign people is an enormous, unending task which should be done slowly and unceasingly. It should begin on the very first day of the study of the foreign language and continue every day thereafter as long as the student is in contact with the language. The task to be done is huge and the time provided for doing it is short. Therefore, the teacher cannot afford not to use almost everything which takes place in and out of the classroom to help him with this complex, many-faceted job.

The best instrument that the teacher has to saturate the student with the culture of the language being taught is the language itself. Language is the mirror of culture. The semantic differences and ranges of any tongue are relevant to its culture. Words make sense only in the terms of the daily life, the customs, the behavior, the attitudes, and the environmental factors and beliefs of the speaker. For true, full comprehension of his language, teacher and student should be concerned with the word of the speaker in the light of the culture of his people.

Every civilization is coherent and every culture is unique and must be understood in terms of its society. The ability must be developed in every foreign language student to see another culture as a reflection of the actions and ideas of another society and not as something which is to be compared with ours. Food, ceremonial rites, prestige, status symbols, family relationships, all material and nonmaterial values must be examined in the terms of the culture of which they are a part. At the door of the foreign language classroom the student should abandon the mentality of his own culture and assume that of the culture he is studying. Everything which he is taught in the language should relate to and be significant of the society which speaks it.

The teacher should take every opportunity to relate language to culture. The student can hardly be expected to gain insight into the way of life of another people if the language he is studying deals with American concepts. A lesson in Spanish which deals with a trip to the Island of Janitzio gives the student better insight into the Spanish language and Mexican culture than a lesson which discusses a trip to the Statue of Liberty. A drill in French which is teaching patterns with the verb "to eat" gives the student more authentic information if the variants are *bouillabaisse, croissants,* and *crêpes suzettes* than if they are apples, pears and plums. Reading about the Ugly Duckling or discussing the celebration of Thanksgiving Day inadequately prepares a student for understanding German culture. It gives him little information about what he can hope to meet when he goes to Germany some day.

The atmosphere as well as the language in the classroom should exude the culture of the people. Authentic gestures, exclamations, expressions; in fact all of the paralinguistic phenomena which can make language come alive should be used whenever and wherever possible. For instance, such gestures as the thumping handshake which French people use when they meet or the typical gesture which Italians use when they say goodbye help to enliven a lesson and create a desirable atmosphere for foreign language learning.

Bookshelves with artifacts and realia, interesting wall displays, dioramas, and murals should be part of the décor in every foreign language classroom (see page 131).

The community can very often provide the teacher with resources of immeasurable value. A consul or a cultural attaché can be called upon to speak, or provide a speaker for club or class meetings. Foreign visitors in the community are often flattered to be asked to meet the students of the foreign language classes. Informal programs provide exciting opportunities for the students to hear the natives use the foreign languages. These occasions also offer the students the chance to use the language which they are studying.

The parents who speak foreign languages are not to be overlooked as valuable resource material in any community. They need not be university trained people in order to make a contribution to the cultural image of their native country. These people are usually very willing to come to class to speak to the students. Such subjects as their childhood or their school days or how the members of the family made a living can provide the learner with information and insight. At such programs, time should be provided for the learner to question the speaker about the way of life in the land where he was born. This exchange of ideas often makes a lasting impression on those who have never been very far from home.

Film showings, songs, dances, and recordings are invaluable for bringing people of other lands closer to the student in the classroom. Every occasion which presents itself and can bring the student into closer contact with the foreign culture should not be neglected or overlooked.

However, these are only the patches in the quilt. Although these isolated items and events stimulate the study of the language they become significant only when they are attached properly to the background to which they belong. The untutored observation of a collection of unrelated items may be misleading, superficial, and even dangerous. To correlate this information intelligently requires a knowledge of the historical background of the country whose language is being taught, as well as a knowledge of the contemporary scene. There is a need to understand the social forces as seen by the sociologists, the economic forces which affect man's conduct, and the culture and civilization which are the foundation upon which all these forces operate.

Since the study of the language must necessarily involve one in the study of people, every foreign language teacher should be required to learn a minimum of basic sociology to gain insight into man's behavior and his reasons for change. Along with sociology the foreign language teacher should be required to study the history of the people and the geography and economics of the land whose language he is teaching. These courses should be taken in the foreign language if possible. If not, they should at least be taken in the other departments which offer them. The acquisition of this knowledge is as important, if not more important, to the student who is preparing to become a language teacher as any of the other kinds of information which he is acquiring. It is as deserving of his time as any of the other courses which are required for earning a degree.

The teacher of a foreign language should also be expected to keep abreast of the contemporary scene by reading the periodicals and journalistic writings of the day. More and more of such current literature is becoming available through direct subscription as well as through importation by American distributors.

Periodically, however, the foreign language teacher needs to recharge his cultural battery at the source of supply. This is particularly true for those instructors who are not in frequent, personal contact with native speakers. Such teachers are limited to their students in their opportunities for communication and to the level and content of the lessons which they teach. It is necessary from time to time to become immersed in the culture of the language one is teaching, to live among the people and to speak with them. Nothing compares with first-hand experiences. Enthusiasm is engendered for many teaching years to come by a trip abroad. Traveling also provides the occasion to obtain those objects, artifacts, pictures, books, etc. which can become so important to the teaching process. Students, too, become more interested in this realia when they know that these materials were obtained through the personal experience of their teacher.

The United States government recognizes the necessity for these voyages. A ruling of the Bureau of Internal Revenue allows a teacher of a foreign language to deduct from his tax return the expenses of a trip abroad to the land whose language he is teaching. No formal study in any institution or university abroad need be involved. To be exposed to the culture of the land whose language one is teaching is the only condition which is required.

THE CULTURAL APPROACH AND THE STUDENT

Gaining an awareness, at a distance, of another culture must necessarily be a slow and lengthy process. It cannot be accomplished by learning the names of the monuments nor by recognizing its masterpieces in art and music. It cannot be achieved by reading one or even two books on the subject. Learning to know a culture is never finished, it goes on long after the formal study of the language is completed.

The more the student sees, hears, and relates, the clearer will become his impressions and ideas. The information necessary for him to reflect upon will come from many sources. The language which he is learning as well as the teacher and the resources he commands should provide part of this cultural information. It is what the student finds out for himself, however, which will probably make the greatest impact on him. Assignments and projects which are calculated to make him secure information through which he will gain insight into the culture of another people, should become part of his language study.

Continuous self-selected readings and related activities should help him gather much pertinent information about other people and their way of life (see page 107). The projects of his classmates, their demonstrations and reports should add to his information about other aspects of the culture and civilization he is seeking to understand. Individual efforts such as contributions to the bulletin board or the pictorial displays in the classroom, or the preparation of a scrap book or a log can help to give him an awareness of the foreign land.

A class project should serve as a cooperative effort in which each member makes a contribution within the limits of his own capacity and through which the whole class gains insight into some aspect of the foreign culture. The construction of a mural, for example, can become such a group undertaking. This kind of cumulative activity can engage the attention and involve the talents and efforts of the entire class over an extended period of time. Students who are artistic, those who like to work in the library, those who prefer to do things with their hands can all participate in this endeavor by contributing their individual talents and efforts. They will learn as they perform.

A mural may take as long as a term to complete. The ideas for the various elements to be depicted can be based on the units which are studied in class. The information needed to render the scenes as authentic as possible can be obtained by all members of the class from books, magazines, and pictures. The execution of the drawings and the design can be the responsibility of the artistic members. The other kinds of construction can be entrusted to the mechanically inclined classmates, the ones who express themselves well provide the text for the explanations and the captions. The execution of the mural should supply each student with the medium for his favorite activity through which he can also accumulate cultural information.

A diorama or some other kind of construction is another class project through which the student can gain much cultural perception. He needs to acquire definite information while he is engaged in the production of these three-dimensional panoramas. The combined efforts of the members of the class can create a very authentic reproduction.

Direct correspondence is an excellent way of obtaining information about other people. Contact through letters between American and foreign students of the same age who have some common interests can become an exciting experience. The correspondence can begin between classes. Using an outline or cue words, the letter to be written can become an exercise for the entire class. This cooperative effort will involve every student and insure that a correct communication will be sent abroad.

As the class increases its ability to handle the written lan-

guage, individual students here and abroad may establish correspondence between themselves. In order to make certain that the
language is correct they should be urged to write about the life
situations they have learned to handle in the units studied in
class.

The contents of the letters received from abroad by the
class or the individual should be shared with and discussed by
the entire class. Information and ideas which emerge from these
discussions will add much to the fund of cultural knowledge the
class is acquiring.

The pen-pal project has been in existence for many years.
Many lasting friendships which started with an exchange of such
letters have been formed between American and foreign students.

Another, more modern, more exciting medium for social intercourse is the sound recording. "Tape-pals" talk to each other
by exchanging sound tapes. The spoken message is more personal, less formal than the written word. The tapes, like the exchange of letters, can be initiated between classes. The performance is better here, too, if the subject matter is selected from the
"real life" units which have been studied and if the contents to
be recorded are drilled as exercises in the classroom.

Participation will keep enthusiasm high. The preparation of
the script should be the cooperative activity of all the members
of the class. Each one should be encouraged to contribute something to it. The recording, too, should reflect the efforts of every
member of the class. Sentences which are assigned to each student may require several rehearsals. Sound effects, songs, and
musical selections can be included to provide the occasion for
some members of the class to display their special talents. A dry
run will help to produce a smooth, correct recording.

The recordings which are received from abroad should become the basis for many classroom activities. In order to derive
as much comprehension as possible from these tapes they should
be played several times. A few lessons should be devoted to listening to the content, followed by questions and answers and
discussions. The cultural allusions should be emphasized and explained wherever possible.

Other exercises such as summaries and retelling might follow when the recording is understood by everyone. Several short dictations based on the contents might also be possible.

In this day of easy and inexpensive photography one can add pictures to letters and to sound tapes to give the receiver an even more complete message. The correspondents will learn to recognize each other by sight. They will see the other members of the class as well as the teacher. They will even be able to visit inside each other's classrooms.

The speaker-phone and the tele-lecture are two of the latest efforts to effect direct communication between groups of people. These electronic instruments make possible conversation between groups who are quite distant from each other. The arrangements for these conversations must be made well in advance and must be well organized. Although contact through these devices is still in the experimental stage there is an elementary school in New York State where students have had several long distance conversations with children in an elementary school in Ecuador. This social intercourse was made through interpreters. The possibilities for the future, however, for foreign language students are very thrilling.

In spite of all the new, exciting kinds of contact described above the best way to get to know and to understand other people is to visit them in their native land. More and more opportunities to travel abroad are being offered to young American students. Junior year abroad, student exchange programs, summer camps abroad, and various experiments in international living are giving many students the chance to live and study in foreign lands. There are also many programs which bring foreign students to our land and to our schools.

The students who have traveled as well as the foreign students who are visiting us have a great deal to offer the rest of the student body. They should be used as often as possible as resource people to give cultural information about the land and the people they have come to know.

CULTURE AND THE LANGUAGE CLUB

A club will rarely attract members unless it offers them activity and excitement. Since attendance is voluntary few students will continue to come if their club activities are a mere repetition of the work they do in the classroom. The club should belong to the students, not to the teacher. The teacher should be there only to advise and guide. The student, however, should profit by his activities in a foreign language club by adding to his fund of cultural knowledge.

Involvement engenders enthusiasm. The student who evinces enough interest to become a member of a language club is indicating a desire to become a participant in its activities. He will continue to come if he is given an active role in its organization and its program. A "showy" project, one which receives acclaim by the school population as well as the community, will attract members to the club. The ego of an organization like that of a human being is nurtured by recognition by others. Confining the activities of a club to the four walls of a classroom does not provide a very exciting prospect to a future member.

The music club has the concert toward which its members bend all their efforts. The drama club has its presentation, the art club its exhibition. The foreign language club, too, could have its day in the limelight. It, too, could produce many exciting "spectaculars" to which parents, administrators, and members of the community are invited.

The programs could become fund raisers for worthy causes such as the student exchange program, the language or summer camp, or additions to the foreign language classrooms and libraries. Through these efforts the foreign language program could be extended in many directions. These affairs could also serve as an instrument for publicity on the study of foreign languages and promote good public relations with the community.

A successful program must involve all the members of the club and should attract and engage many new ones. It should give each one a job to do within his capacity. The brilliant and the not so brilliant language students both have a proper place in the language club and both can contribute much to its success. They should each derive pleasure and knowledge from their membership. The program should involve lots of planning by the members, lots of committees with definite jobs to do, lots of publicity inside and outside of school. It should be of such scope and importance that it takes several months to put together. Planning, executing, and publicizing a long-term project produces the momentum of excitement which makes belonging to a club the fun it ought to be.

The full responsibility for these social affairs need not rest entirely on the teacher's shoulders. Majors in foreign languages from nearby colleges or universities, members of university educational societies, and student teachers could be solicited to help with overseeing some of the committee work or other aspects of the preparation and arrangements.

Two or more departments of the school might be willing to combine efforts. Such cooperation should be sought wherever possible. It makes for closer relations between the foreign language department and other departments in the school and it engages a larger segment of the school population in the foreign language project.

Following are some suggestions for spectacular foreign language events. The possibility of carrying out any of these depends, of course, on the facilities which are available to the teacher in the school and the community. The ingenious teacher will think of others which are feasible in his special situation.

A *combined concert and exhibition* could involve the cooperation of the music, art, and language departments. The concert of foreign music could be choral or instrumental or both. The exhibition could be the work of individuals or groups. It could combine two and three dimensional items. Original works or beautiful posters and photographic material taken from foreign magazines make interesting displays.

This would be a good occasion to show student-made murals, dioramas, replicas, and other such artistic creations. Three dimensional objects such as hand-dressed dolls in costume, paper sculptures of monuments, piñatas, and costumes also help make an exhibit a success. Student-made items always are of great interest and pride to the parents and a display of these will serve to attract them to the program.

The concert and the exhibit could each be given one half the allotted time of presentation. The exhibit may be viewed either before or after the concert.

An international fair is always popular with students and grown-ups. The booths of the various nations could offer typical baked-goods and foods as well as small objects for sale. Handmade items which are copies of typical foreign ones are usually easy to sell. The salesclerks and hosts and hostesses could be dressed in costumes. Part of the evening could be devoted to a program of foreign song and dance.

A Christmas program of many lands could be combined with a fair. The program could be devoted to showing how Christmas is celebrated in the various countries of the world. In conjunction with such a program typical Christmas foods could be displayed and sold. Such a fair held before Christmas offers the audiences the opportunity to buy Christmas gifts of their own.

An international banquet where a menu of foods from many lands is served could be brought about through the combined efforts of the home economics and foreign language departments. Each guest could be provided with a souvenir program with footnotes about the origin of the various offerings. A program of song and dance as the entertainment of the evening could give the guests an added attraction for their money.

An international variety show offers an opportunity for many different types of entertainment by individuals and groups. To the usual songs and dances and music could be added slide talks by students who have been recipients of awards who have traveled abroad or have been to a language camp. Visiting foreign students could be asked to give a slide talk about their native land. Visiting students should always be asked to come prepared with illustrative material for lectures. Community singing, with words of the songs flashed on the screen is usually very popular.

An audience should be given a printed program and program notes for every program. The content of these notes should be the result of research done by a committee and should give the audience correct pertinent cultural information about what they are seeing and hearing.

The language club, if properly motivated, can provide students with meaningful and purposeful activity as well as fun and excitement. It can also create a stir of excitement in the school and in the community. And that, after all, is what a student is looking for when he joins a club.

CULTURE AND LITERATURE

One of the reasons most frequently advanced for the study of literary masterpieces is that good literature gives the reader insight into the cultural patterns of a society. This is a spurious argument since the piece of writing which has become a classic has probably attained that lofty place in the literary world for several other reasons. The stylistic ingenuity of the author, his personal philosophy, or a situation which has universal implications in all societies are more likely to be reflected in his writing than his observations of the usual, routine things of life in any one society.

All works of fiction are wholly or at best partly the result of someone's imagination. The characters tend to be cultural stereotypes rather than real personalities. The sociological and economic conditions of the story have been created by the author. The interaction of fictitious characters in invented situations cannot serve the student to interpret real patterns of social and economic behavior.

Furthermore, the concentration on literary pieces several decades, and in some cases several centuries old, presents the student with a picture of a society which no longer exists and one which he may be led to believe erroneously is a reflection of the present cultural picture.

Articles in popular magazines and second-rate novels which will probably never attain any great level of distinction for writing style are likely to yield more culturally pertinent matter than literary prize-winners. Advertisements, journalistic reportage, surveys, and monographs in the hands of qualified teachers can be more valuable as social documents than the literary landmarks of the same era.

Literature should be read for beauty of style and language, for the imagination and creation of the author and not for an evaluation of the behavioral patterns of a society as seen through the actions of the fictional characters.

Such a sociological assessment cannot reflect the true culture of a people. On the contrary it may be the basis for dangerous stereotyping or serious misinformation.

The cultural aspect of foreign language instruction is indeed complicated and demanding. It requires time, creativity and imagination on the part of the teacher and the student. However, the ingenious instructor and the curious, inquiring student, are both rewarded for their efforts. It is precisely this aspect of language education that makes up for the necessary tedium of repetition and drills and exercises.

The cultural approach and the activities related to it are what can make the acquisition of a language a stimulating and exhilarating experience. The teacher who neglects this aspect of language instruction is depriving his students of a vital ingredient for interested learning. He is also depriving himself of the experience of having eager, enthusiastic students.

SUGGESTED READINGS:

Benedict, Ruth, *Patterns of Culture* (New York, New American Library, 1959).

Lewald, Ernest H., "Problems in Culture Teaching," *The Modern Language Journal*, Vol. 47, No. 6, Oct. 1963.

Northeast Conference on the Teaching of Foreign Languages, "Culture in Language Learning," Reports of the Working Committees, 1960.

Vargas, Enrique, "The Jet-Age Malady," *Saturday Review*, May 29, 1965.

FOR INFORMATION

On Exchange Students:

American Field Service, 113 East 30th St., New York, N.Y. 10016.

American Friends Service Committee, 20 S. 12th St., Philadelphia, Pa. 19107.

Experiment in International Living, Putney, Vt. 05346.

Institute of International Education, 809 United Nations Plaza, Second Ave., New York, N.Y. 10017.

Pan American Union, 17th St. & Constitution Ave., N. W. Washington D.C. 20037.

On Pen-Pals:

Letters Abroad, 18 East 60th St., New York, N.Y. 10022.

Bureau de Correspondance Scolaire, Director Frances V. Guille, College of Wooster, Wooster, Ohio.

International Friendship League, 40 Mt. Vernon St., Boston, Mass. 02108.

Office of Private Cooperation, U.S. Information Agency, 1776 Pennsylvania Ave. N.W., Washington, D.C. 20006.

Oficina Nacional de Correspondencia, Escolar, Director Harley D. Oberhelman, Dept. of Foreign Languages, Texas Technological College, Lubbock, Tex. 79406.

On Sources for Cultural Materials (all languages):

MLA, "Selective List of Materials For Use by Teachers of Modern Foreign Languages in Elementary and Secondary Schools," Modern Language Association, 4 Washington Place, New York, N.Y. 10003.

Eaton, Esther, *et al.,* "Source Materials for Secondary School Teachers of Foreign Languages," Bulletin 1962 (OE-27001 B), U.S. Department of Health, Education, and Welfare, Office of Education, Washington, D.C. 20202.

On Study Abroad:

Europcentres, Erhard J. C. Waespi, Director, Seestrasse 247, Zurich 2/38 Switzerland.

Abrams, Irwin, "Study Abroad," Bulletin No. 6 (OE-50016), U.S. Department of Health, Education, and Welfare, Office of Education, Washington 6, D.C., 1960.

UNESCO, "Study Abroad," Bulletin No. 13, 1961–1962, UNESCO Publications Center, 801 Third Ave., New York, N.Y. 10022.

On Student Travel:

Council on Student Travel, Inc., 179 Broadway, New York, N.Y. 10007.

The Council on Student Travel, 777 United Nations Plaza, New York, N.Y. 10017.

Educational Travel, Inc., 265 Madison Ave., New York, N.Y. 10016.

American Youth Hostels, 14 West 8th St., New York, N.Y. 10011.

The Commission on Youth Service Projects, 475 Riverside Drive (Room 825), New York, N.Y. 10027.

On Tape-Pals:

International Tape Exchange, Ruth Terry, 834 Reiddman Ave., No. Muskegon, Mich. 49445.

The Voicespondence Club, Noel, Va.

World Tape Pals, Inc., Box 9211, Dallas 15, Tex.

S.T.E.P. (German Tape Exchange), Carl D. Bauer, 1713 Sherwood Rd., New Cumberland, Pa. 17070.

9
MEASURING ACHIEVEMENT

- Tests are essential to measure the teacher's effectiveness as well as the student's achievement.
- Tests, to be efficacious, should be fair and well-constructed.
- There are good tests for measuring oral and audio skills.
- Printed tests can reflect efficiency only in the graphic skills.

Both learner and teacher need some means of determining the success of the instruction. Tests should evaluate the teacher's effectiveness as well as the pupil's knowledge. If the majority of the students have not learned well enough to pass the test, it should be clear that the material was not taught cogently and needs to be re-taught. Those whose test results show that they did not understand the material, should be helped to perceive it.

In the area of testing, as in all other areas of language learning, the student and teacher must establish a friendly rapport. Tests should be fair. They should be designed to find out what the student knows and not to frustrate or trap him. They should provide a sense of achievement for the majority of the class. A fair test will encourage and motivate the student. An unfair test may turn him against the teacher and the entire foreign language program. Satisfactory results reward a student for his efforts and give him a sense of accomplishment. There is no better lift for the ego than to receive recognition for achievement. There is no better method for spurring the student on to continued endeavor.

SOME GENERAL PRINCIPLES FOR GOOD AND FAIR TESTS

1. *Never give an unannounced test.* The teacher who "springs" tests creates an atmosphere of apprehension in the classroom. The student is never sure of what is in store for him when he enters the room. A test should always be announced in advance. The subject matter should be properly reviewed in class and assigned for study at home prior to the presentation of the test.

However, very short daily quizzes need not be announced every time if it is made clear at the beginning of the term that everyone is responsible every day for yesterday's lesson. These short, one-topic exams are good for keeping the student alert and for quick reviews of the most recently taught material.

2. *Do not fail to give the examination at the scheduled time and test only those items you indicated you would test.* The student must be able to trust you and depend on your word. Do not include topics for which he has not been told in advance to prepare. Only those structures which have been mastered should be tested and those structures which are tested should be weighted so as to reflect the relative importance which they were given in the lesson. For instance, a point which was glossed over or mentioned casually in class should not become an important question on the test. If he feels that you do not keep your word the student may be reluctant to prepare for your examinations. He may even decide not to prepare for them at all.

3. *Make your directions very clear.* It is unfair to penalize the student who may know the answer but does not understand the instructions. The directions given on a test should be the same as those the student has heard many times in class. Confronting him with orders which he has never heard before might give him a feeling of anxiety which could prevent him from showing what he really knows. Give several examples to further clarify what you expect the student to do. Use the same techniques and questioning devices in testing that you have used in teaching. Be as reasonable, clear, and concise as possible. Good instructions and familiar procedures help to get a test started

smoothly and promptly without interruptions from those who need more explanations.

4. *Give many short quizzes.* Test one thing at a time and keep the test short. Frequent short quizzes on individual structures which have been thoroughly taught, drilled, and mastered are very essential to the instructional process. A quiz should be given when the teacher has finished teaching a topic. The results will indicate to him whether or not it has been learned. If it has been mastered by the class, he is ready to move on to the next topic; if it has not, he will need to spend some more time drilling it. Although the quiz should be kept short, the number of questions should be sufficient to cover the subject and of the right degree of difficulty so that the student will have ample opportunity to show that he has learned. The frequent, short quiz provides the teacher with many grades for each student and consequently with a better profile of his work. The quiz which tests only one item takes little time to give and is quick and easy to mark. Test papers should be returned as soon after the quiz as possible while the questions are still fresh in the student's mind and his interest is high.

5. *Avoid giving full period tests.* Tests which cover several topics are needed from time to time to discover how much and how well the student has retained what has been taught. However, these tests should be so designed that they do not consume the entire period. Enough time should be allowed for reviewing the answers to the questions before the class leaves the room.

Departmental, state, regional, or standardized tests should be the only extra-long tests which are given. The teacher, without doubt, will not be able to examine the questions in these tests with the class the day they are given. However, if the student is to learn and profit from his mistakes such tests should not go by without review. They should be discussed as soon as possible after they have been taken.

6. *Review answers immediately after the test.* The answers to the questions should be given immediately after the test papers have been collected. This is precisely the moment when the students are curious and anxious to learn the correct answers.

Testing should reinforce learning and it is inefficient to let that peak moment of curiosity go by without satisfying the student's desire to discover if he has learned correctly. This procedure also insures immediate correction of an incorrect response. Another review of the answers should take place when the test papers are returned. This time the student should correct his answer on his paper if it needs correction.

7. *Use material which resembles normal speech.* Test vocabulary and structures in context only. Make up sentences which are most likely to be said or written. Keep the test entirely in the foreign language (see page 24). If you use the same directions on the test that you use in class there will be no need to give directions in English.

8. *Design the test so that it measures achievement in the area you are seeking to examine.* The answers of a test should reveal its purpose. Written tests cannot reflect oral proficiency. Oral tests cannot provide a barometer for measuring correct written form. A test intended to evaluate pronunciation should not be used to evaluate structure and grammar. Try to answer the questions of the test yourself to see if it does what you want it to do and if it elicits the answers you are seeking.

When going over the answers of a written test make sure that the students see the correct written form. Write the answers on the board. Giving the answers orally to a written test does not insure graphic perception of the correct form by the student.

TESTING AUDIO AND ORAL SKILLS

Testing method and purpose go hand in hand. In the areas of aural comprehension and speaking the tests must be designed to measure achievement in the audio and oral skills.

Some educational achievement is not easy to measure. For instance, the skill of comprehension of the spoken word is more easily measurable than the degree of achievement in the ability to speak.

The ability to speak encompasses competence in several areas, each of which is important in producing good spoken language. In measuring achievement and proficiency in oral skill several components must be taken into consideration separately if the student is to profit from the results of his tests.

To evaluate the speech of a student a teacher must examine four elements.

- His ability to produce the sounds of the foreign language.
- His ability to produce these sounds fluently and in the correct phrases and groupings.
- His ability to emphasize the correct syllables in these group- ings.
- His ability to properly intone the whole utterance.

Inaccuracy in any one of these elements will render the whole production faulty. In other words, when one is measuring achievement in the ability to speak, the teacher must consider the four elements of *pronunciation, fluency, stress,* and *intonation* and must analyze each one separately in his notebook. Such anal- ysis enables the teacher to give help in those areas where the stu- dent needs it most.

Speaking is the most difficult area to test because no stand- ardized instrument has as yet been invented which a teacher can use to isolate and test the four elements of speech. The test on tape, although not standardized, does give the teacher some kind of vehicle for examining the spoken language of his students. The tape makes it possible to listen to each student's recording several times for an appraisal of the various speech elements.

Tape tests can be given to an entire class easily and quickly in the language laboratory. It is possible, however, to give these recorded tests in the classroom with the use of one tape recorder. An easy way to administer a test on tape is to set a microphone up on the teacher's desk. Students are called up one at a time to answer a question or two which is asked either by the teacher or a recording on another machine. The entire class can be taped in a very short time.

When scoring this kind of test, whether given in the lan- guage laboratory or the classroom, the teacher should listen for only one element in the student responses, such as one sound, the intonation pattern, or the fluency. A sufficient number of tests on tape should give the teacher a very good overall evaluation of the student's oral ability. A taped test takes a longer time to score but it does provide a record of student performance which an oral test cannot do. Speech production tests, whether taped or oral, are largely dependent on the subjective decision of the teacher.

The simplest test for speech production is the echo test which requires the student to imitate what he hears. Although this does show how well the student can produce the foreign sounds it does not show how he controls his own flow of language without a model. The best techniques for testing spoken language are those which evoke the normal use and pace of language.

A test in which a student tells what he sees in a simple picture is good for measuring his own spontaneous performance. The picture should be simple and uncluttered and could even be one which the student has seen and used before.

A test which requires the student to complete an unfinished statement is another way of evoking normal speech. A series of simple questions which require answers is still another device for evaluating control of spoken language. On these tests the oral performance and not the content of the utterance should be judged. Tests which are devised to concentrate on one phonemic phenomenon at a time enable the teacher to analyze the student's speech and to help him with the required remedial exercises.

Reading aloud is not a good method for testing oral competence because reading and speaking are not parallel skills. Many factors connected with reading can affect what the student says and may not necessarily be a measure of his capacity to produce speech. His physical ability to see the written word clearly, grasp its meaning, translate the written symbol into its spoken form, and the actual eye movements all affect the act of reading. None of these, however, has anything to do with the ability to produce speech well.

TESTING AUDIO SKILLS

In measuring aural comprehension there are two dimensions with which the teacher must be concerned. One refers to discrimination between sounds, and the other refers to understanding the meaning of the spoken language. Tests for distinguishing sounds should center around the recognition of phonemes. In the pre-reading period, before the student can write the foreign word, paper and pencil tests can be devised in which he indicates by some kind of mark whether he can hear the difference between sounds.

For instance, several sentences can be spoken, some of which contain the phoneme to be identified and some of which do not. The teacher announces the number of each sentence as he pronounces it. The student writes on a sheet of paper the number of the sentence which contains the desired phoneme. Other tests might ask the student to count the number of times he hears a phoneme in a sentence which the teacher or a record or tape pronounces.

After the student has learned to write the foreign word, there are many other ways of ascertaining if he can recognize the sounds of the language. He might be given a spot dictation in which he is required to complete sentences with words contain- ing the target sound. He might be given two columns of words in which he is asked to match those which contain the same sounds. Or he might be asked to underline similar phonemes which appear in different sentences.

Other tests might require recognition of phonemic differences. For instance a spot dictation in French might require the student to fill in the blank with words which he hears. This would contain *ou* and *u*. *La* roue *est petite mais la* rue *est grande.* In Spanish the exercise might contain words with *r* or *rr*. *El* perro *ladra* pero *nadie entiende.* The student would have to be able to distinguish between these sounds in order to select the correct one.

The other aspect, that of comprehension for meaning, is easier to evaluate. The best test for proving comprehension is the one where the student cannot depend on the structure of the question for his answer. In the pre-reading period, different kinds of picture tests provide the teacher with good paper and pencil tests for comprehension. The students check pictures which apply to the spoken statements given by the teacher. There is no need to write any words and there is no way of depending on the question for the answer. For instance a picture of a kitchen and a picture of a bedroom are drawn on a sheet of paper. Several statements are made which can refer to what one sees or does in either of these rooms. The student is required to check the picture to which the statements relate; or numbered statements may be made about both pictures. The students would have to place the correct numbers under the picture to which they refer.

Sometimes even comprehension of structures can be tested by pictures. For instance, the teacher can say, "the map is on the chair," and the student has to choose from among three pictures which show a map *on the chair,* one *under the chair* and a third one *over the chair.*

Other tests for comprehension can be used in which such signs as + for true and − for false are written about statements which the student hears read by a teacher or a machine.

Action response tests for aural comprehension are particularly well-suited to the pre-reading period. In these tests students are given directions orally and they respond by performing. The teacher can then determine whether the student understands by the way he performs or fails to perform correctly. Such multiple directions as "go to the window and count up to five" or "hold out your right hand and open your book with your left" show a teacher whether or not a student understands what he hears.

Some action response tests can be given to groups as well as to individuals. The command "Raise your right hand" to the whole class may reveal easily and quickly the student who does not perform correctly because he does not understand.

Other tests for the pre-reading period can require the student to act out what he hears described in a short story which the teacher reads aloud. Vocabulary tests could require the student to take items from a box as they are referred to by the teacher, or to point to various real or pictured objects as they are spoken about by the teacher or one of the students in the class. It is important to remember not to make vocabulary tests a listing of words. Lexical items should be given in context only.

Many tests for aural comprehension can be turned into guessing games. Such games as "What is it?" or "Where is it?" if the teacher gives several appropriate clues test comprehension and provide fun at the same time.

After the pre-reading period, the teacher has various other kinds of tests to choose from for evaluating aural comprehension. The most usual is the question and answer type. Here again, as in the pre-reading period, it is better to formulate a question which cannot be used by the student for his answer. For instance, "Is M. Dupont at home?" can be answered using most of the language of the question for the answer. "Yes, M. Dupont is at home." This answer can be made by some students by taking it right out of the mouth of the teacher without really understanding either the question or the answer. A better question is "Where is M. Dupont?" because the student must understand what he hears if he is to answer correctly.

Multiple choice questions, true-false, or completion questions can be used for verifying comprehension. Summaries, and selection of cue phrases and sentences are good devices for measuring understanding of what the student hears.

TESTING READING

The tests for reading should be concerned with how much comprehension the student has derived from the printed page. The techniques one can use are much the same as those which were used for verifying comprehension from the spoken word.

Multiple choice and true-false tests can be used as well as the question-answer type test. Here, even more than in aural comprehension, the teacher must devise the kinds of questions which will require the student to think about the answer, one which he is not likely to find by simply trying to match the words of the question to the words he finds on the printed page.

Summaries, resumés, choosing clue words, and making an outline are all good methods for proving that a student has come away with clear ideas of the material he has read. All of the devices discussed in the chapter on reading can be used as testing devices (see page 105).

TESTING WRITING

Writing tests are usually concerned primarily with such items as structure, form, and vocabulary. How well one writes depends on how well one knows the form. Guided writing or writing of compositions is more likely to be treated as classwork or homework and not as a test. Where a student is required to write a composition either cued or free as a test, style or originality will suffer if there is no correctness of structure and form.

In writing tests concerned with vocabulary, structure or syntax, it is best to give the student the kind of test which does not present him with more than one difficulty at a time. He should have a clear idea of the subject being tested. After taking the test, he should have a good idea of how well he knows the items tested or what he needs to study in order to gain control of them.

Questions which test writing should be presented to the student in written form and not orally. They should be mimeographed on the test paper itself or written on the board. Dictating the questions of a test is unfair. It presents the student with writing difficulties that have nothing to do with the material which is being tested. Furthermore presenting the written questions to the students makes it possible for them to get promptly started on the test itself without creating any pre-test confusion.

Vocabulary should never be tested in lists. The meaning of words should be delivered in context. The test should be so designed that the student has to make a choice from several contextual situations. For instance, a test in French might read:

> *Jean écrit avec*   1. *un cahier.*
>   2. *un écriteau.*
>   3. *un stylo à bille.*

One in Spanish might be:

> *Usamos una llave*   1. *para llevar los libros.*
>   2. *para lavar la ropa.*

3. *para jugar a las cartas.*
4. *para cerrar la puerta.*

Until the student becomes very proficient in handling the written language, the tests on syntax or structure should require him to insert only a word or two in a sentence. Wherever possible in written or oral testing, grammatical terminology should be kept to a minimum. It is more meaningful to use expressions of function. Emphasizing usage helps to reinforce learning and to crystallize the purpose of the test.

For instance, instead of saying "Change all the following sentences to the future tense" it is more purposeful to say "Use the word 'tomorrow' in each of the following sentences and make the appropriate changes."

Or, instead of saying "Insert the proper form of the disjunctive pronouns in the blanks" the student will learn more about usage and will be less bewildered if he is asked to "Insert the proper form of the pronouns after the prepositions in the following sentences."

As the student becomes more skilled in the manipulation and use of the foreign language, he can be expected to write larger and larger segments of it with fewer cues and guides from the teacher. Many of the suggestions in the chapter on writing may be also used as testing devices (see page 113).

Where programmed material has been used for practice and drill (see page 91) it could be used subsequently for testing. This technique not only tests but also reinforces learning because the step-by-step emphasis of the design gives the student immediate information on the correctness of his response.

Testing should provide a periodic measurement of what the student has learned. It should become a barometer for indicating continuing progress and growth. It is a rare student who is not anxious to better his score. Apathy sets in only when he feels frustrated, trapped, and unable to improve. Tests should be so designed as to encourage even the slowest student. Good, fair tests in which each student feels a sense of achievement will contribute greatly to building favorable attitudes and to sustaining interest and enthusiasm in continuing the study of the language.

SUGGESTED READINGS:

Brooks, Nelson, *Language and Language Learning: Theory and Practice* (New York, Harcourt, Brace & World, 1960).

Lado, Robert, *Language Testing: The Construction and Use of Foreign Language Tests* (New York, McGraw-Hill, 1964).

10

THE FOREIGN LANGUAGE CONTINUUM

- The amount of school time in which the student is expected to acquire the skills of a foreign language is ridiculously low.
- The student is best suited physiologically to begin foreign language instruction before he reaches the age of eight.
- The time for foreign language instruction can be increased by including this discipline in the elementary school curriculum.
- The student can only benefit from his experience with a foreign langauge if he is carried through from the elementary school to the senior high school in a continuous well-articulated course of study.
- Articulation can be achieved if supervision and instruction is vertical, cutting through all levels.

It takes years to learn to control the four skills of a foreign language. Calculated in terms of hours, the amount of contact time a student is given with foreign language instruction is ridiculously low.

Experience with children repeatedly demonstrates that they learn languages more quickly than adults. Physiologists tell us that the best age for imitation is somewhere between six and eight years of age. It is also at this age that children are least inhibited and delight in learning new sounds and new skills. After eight years of age this capacity steadily decreases and the child is apt to become more analytical and less expansive and receptive to language learning.

Obviously then, if we are to take advantage of the child's

innate capacity for learning and if we are to be realistic about the amount of time one needs for acquiring the skills of a foreign language, we should start to teach second languages at the age of six or seven. Although some Americans view this as a very revolutionary idea in education, it has long been the practice in many European countries to start teaching children their first foreign language at the age of seven and to add one or two others shortly thereafter. Indeed, it is most wasteful of a child's best years for language learning to start him in his second language at the age of twelve or thirteen when he is no longer at his best to initiate this study.

FOREIGN LANGUAGES IN THE
ELEMENTARY SCHOOL (FLES)

FLES programs in the U.S. follow one of several patterns.

Many school districts subscribe to FLES programs which are taught over television. The lessons are given by a foreign language specialist for about fifteen minutes twice or three times a week. The follow-up procedures vary greatly from district to district. They range from regular visits by competent foreign language specialists to no follow-up at all between tele-lessons.

Another pattern for FLES instruction provides qualified foreign language instructors who teach all the students in a particular school district from the fourth grade on. The instruction usually takes place twice or three times a week for about twenty minutes. These teachers are required to travel from school to school and from classroom to classroom.

Still another pattern is a community-sponsored program which meets after school once a week. Usually the instruction is in the hands of a native speaker who is not necessarily a qualified teacher of the subject.

Some FLES programs are taught by classroom teachers who have had very little, if any, language training. They are studying the language as they are teaching it to the children. There are many correlated audio and visual materials available to help the teacher with this instruction.

FLES programs usually start in the fourth grade. Sometimes

the course is offered to all the children in that grade and the poor ones are then weeded out in the fifth grade. More often it is offered only to those children who have high IQ's and high reading scores. The schedule usually calls for fifteen or twenty minute periods twice or three times a week.

If FLES is to fulfill the function for which it is intended, it should be the beginning of a serious, continuing program. It should become an integral part of the curriculum and the school day.

The author conducted a project under a grant from the University of Pennsylvania in which two schedules of FLES were studied in three elementary schools in and near Philadelphia, Pennsylvania. One schedule gave foreign language instruction to fourth grade students for thirty minute periods twice a week (the normal schedule). The other involved the students every day for twelve minute periods (dividing the allotted hour into a weekly program of regular daily contact time).

The conclusions revealed startling differences in attitudes toward foreign language learning and performance by the students, the classroom teachers, and the community. The twelve minute groups were more enthusiastic about their foreign language experience than were the other groups. They used the language out of class, in the halls, and on the playground whenever they could, and they were excited about continuing the study of the language.

The acquisition of foreign language skills requires regular practice. This study should be included in the child's daily schedule. The program should start him off with the kind of foreign language education which will provide him with a good foundation for future instruction. It should articulate with the language instruction which he is to receive when he leaves the elementary school and goes on to the next higher level.

THE PROBLEMS OF ARTICULATION

The acquisition of foreign language skills requires time and continuity. One year of classwork can hardly be equated with a calendar year. The time allotted during the entire scholastic year to the study of a foreign language is actually less than the amount of time a man spends eating lunch over a six-month period. The average class period per day is less than an hour and the average school year is about 180 days.

Ideally the foreign language program should start in the fourth grade and carry the child through in an unbroken stream of instruction to the twelfth grade. The whole program should be integrated so that the skills which are taught at one level are strengthened and reinforced at the next level. Only in such a continuum can the student benefit from an early start and receive enough experience in foreign language study to acquire the skills necessary to control it. Then the colleges and universities would receive language students who would be qualified to undertake the calibre of language studies one should expect to find in those institutions of higher learning.

Articulation between levels, the elementary school, the junior high school, and the senior high school, is one of the thorniest problems in many school districts and a great deterrent to an effective foreign language program. This is equally true of the colleges and universities which receive students from the lower schools. The difficulties in the school districts stem from several quarters:

1. There is a lack of clear communication among the various levels. In some districts the teachers never meet together to discuss questions which affect all students of the district. In many cases they only hear of each other through the stories which the students carry back and forth between the schools.

2. The courses of study are chosen separately for each level, and there is no agreement on overall aims and goals for the entire curriculum. Consequently, students from a lower level who enter with audio and lingual skills are frustrated in classes on the next level which are translation-grammar oriented. There are even instances where senior high school teachers refuse to accept what the student has learned in junior high school and start him all over again from the beginning. Such practices can only result in disappointment and dissatisfaction.

3. There is a lack of understanding of the problems which are particular to each level. The senior high school teacher is not likely to understand the behavioral patterns of the junior high school student

which must affect the teacher's treatment of him. The FLES teacher would hardly recognize his young student when he reaches the junior high or senior high school level. This lack of perception often leads to an attitude of disdain or disrespect between teachers of the several levels.

As long as the various levels remain isolated from one another, each one functioning independently without regard or responsibility for any of the others, the problem of articulation will persist. Instruction of a foreign language must be thought of as a continuous process. The student who embarks on this study must be assured that he will be able to pursue and complete it without hiatus, unnecessary setbacks, or regressions. Such frustrations are unfair to the student and they are detrimental to the whole foreign language program.

LOOKING TOWARD THE HORIZON

If the student is to be given continuous, correlated instruction there must be a single syllabus for the entire program of instruction which he is to receive. Ideally this course of study should carry the student from the elementary grade through the high school. If there is no FLES program, the course should carry him from the junior high through the senior high school.

Instead of having a foreign language department in every school, the school district should maintain a central foreign language department under the supervision of one person. This "vertical" supervisor should be responsible for coordinating and overseeing the program in all its phases on every level and in every school. He should not be required to teach more than two classes so that he has enough time to devote to running the department and supervising the teachers in it.

The syllabus and the materials of instruction should be the result of discussions and considerations of all the foreign language teachers of the entire district. Each instructor would thus be kept aware of what is going on in all parts of the system. He would see clearly how what he does in his classroom fits into the total program. He would also feel the responsibility for forging a strong link in the chain, which will carry the student on to the next link.

When the aims and goals of the program are decided on after discussion by all the foreign language teachers of the district, the materials should be chosen to implement and carry forth those principles. Every one would then be going in the same direction. The student would not be confronted sometime during his course with practices he was not taught, which he is incapable of handling, and which set him back in his studies.

Carrying the idea of a unified foreign language department a step further, it would be entirely feasible to have teachers move back and forth from level to level. The senior high school teacher would profit greatly from teaching occasionally in the FLES program or in the junior high school. It is conceivable to have teachers scheduled for more than one level in one term. Such vertical programming can have many advantages.

1. It would break down the barriers between levels and schools. Foreign language instructors would not be labeled junior high or senior high or FLES but simply teachers of the language they teach.

2. It would make each teacher responsible for the whole program. The department's problems would become everybody's business. One level could not blame the other level for sending unprepared students ahead.

3. It would provide supervision for every level. Often in a school district with but one or two junior high schools, each with one teacher, there is no provision for supervision of that level. This is equally true of the FLES teacher who is the only one in the district. These teachers are left to their own devices. They are called upon to make their own syllabus and choose their own materials which they do without competent guidance and direction.

A vertical supervisor would be ready to assist these teachers with any problem which would arise. The junior high and FLES teachers especially are in critical positions since they teach beginning language courses. They need someone to turn to for advice and counsel.

4. There would be someone available and responsible for giving in-service training where it is necessary. In-service courses on methods would be required of every teacher and not just one segment of the teaching population of the school district.

The foreign language supervisor who gives workshops or in-service courses should make the distinction between those courses which relate to the use of a publisher's set of materials and those which are concerned with methods applicable to all materials. The former should not be labelled as methods courses but as "How to teach with such and such materials." These distinctions will help the uninitiated teachers to differentiate between the approach and the materials.

5. There would be fewer split programs. If teachers were teaching their own language on more than one level it would be easier to schedule full one-language programs. This might necessitate traveling between two buildings. However, it is easier to do that than to attempt to teach a second foreign language or another subject of which one is not sure and for which one has no enthusiasm.

6. A unified department would make better use of the combined funds of all departments. It could accumulate a professional library of books, periodicals, and materials and avoid duplication by each school. It could provide funds for representatives to go to meetings and conventions more easily than a single school could.

7. A unified foreign language department would be able to provide a supply of teachers for the FLES program of the district. The classes could be divided among several teachers of the department who would teach some FLES along with classes on other levels. In this way students would begin their study of the language with competent instructors. No one teacher would be burdened with an unreasonable teaching load.

Such scheduling would also assure a school district of a continuing FLES program since there would always be teachers available to handle it. The loss of the FLES teacher would not mean the end of the program, as it so often does now.

We are living in historical times, times in which change is inexorable and inevitable. To resist change is to pull down the shades in the classroom and try to shut out the light of the outside world. To hold back change is to vainly hope that if we pay it no mind it will go away and leave us alone. To ignore change is to pretend it does not exist. Any attempt to resist change, hold it back, or ignore it is futile.

However, change just for the sake of change is not necessarily progress. Beware of the change which is merely different and not really better. Do not be stampeded into making the change because others are doing it. Take the time to give careful thought and study to the changes you are considering. Make only those which give access to excellence.

It is the fond hope of the author that this book has given the reader the dimensions against which he can measure the changes he considers for today as well as the horizons against which he can project his contemplations for tomorrow.

SUGGESTED READINGS:

Dellaccio, Carl, "The Six-Year Sequence: Looming Problems and Possible Solutions," *The DFL Bulletin,* Department of Foreign Languages, National Education Association, Vol. 4, No. 1, February, 1965.

Keese, Elizabeth, "Modern Foreign Languages in the Elementary School," Bulletin No. 29 (OE 27007), United States Department of Health, Education, and Welfare, Office of Education, Washington, D.C., 1960.

Moskowitz, Gertrude, *et al.,* "TV FLES and Live FLES," *Modern Language Journal,* Vol. 46, May 1962.

Northeast Conference on the Teaching of Foreign Languages, "The Foreign Language Program—Grades 3 to 12," Reports of the Working Committees, 1956, 1958.

Penfield, Wilder, *et al., Speech and Brain Mechanisms* (Princeton, N.J., Princeton University Press, 1959).

Thompson, Elizabeth, *et al.,* "Foreign Language Teaching in Elementary School," Association for Supervision and Curriculum Development, Washington, D.C., 1958.

APPENDIX A
TIPS

This section is shop talk. Every craftsman is interested in the small talk which concerns the tricks of his trade. The tips which are contained in this section were gained by the author through her own experiences, by observation, and by conversations with many teachers in their classrooms and out of them.

ON CLASSROOM MANAGEMENT AND PROCEDURES

1. Whenever you read or hear about a teaching technique which appeals to you, analyze it carefully first, and as soon as you have a clear idea of how to use it, try it in your classroom. If you delay practicing it you may forget it. If you put it to use immediately and it works well, it may become part of your bag of tricks.

2. Always prepare very detailed lesson plans. You will avoid many mistakes and much embarrassment if you think your lesson through very carefully and look up those items of which you are not sure. Do not trust to luck and your memory to provide you with good examples and variants for your exercises and drills.

Search until you find the best illustrations for your lesson. Pronounce all the sentences aloud to make sure that they will not present phonemic problems which will interfere with their effectiveness.

3. Write the examples you intend to use as well as the drills and their variants on 3 x 5 cards. Establish subject matter headings in the upper left hand corner. In this way you can accumulate a file of good, pertinent items which can be used over and over again. This kind of card system also makes it easy for you to delete those examples which prove not to be effective. A card file also enables you to add to your items whenever you happen to

come across something which you know will serve you when you are ready for it.

4. Assign students to be responsible for erasing all the boards before your class begins. Unrelated material which is sometimes even another language is not a suitable background for the lesson you are teaching.

5. At the beginning of the term establish the general rules for student behavior and classroom organization and stick to them. Such procedures should include the arrangement of written homework, how to enter and leave the room, where to put books and notebooks when oral work is going on, and how to collect tests, homework, and papers. Classroom management will be greatly facilitated if everyone understands and follows the ground rules.

One rule which must be established the very first day of the term is that all speech must be loud and clear enough for everyone to hear. This applies to choral as well as to individual performance. No mumbling should be tolerated. An answer which cannot be heard is to be considered an incorrect answer. (Taking the notebook in your hand and pretending to mark a few such inaudible utterances is one way to help your students find their voices.)

If from time to time a student should forget to speak up, let the class help you to remind him. He will be more responsive to their admonition than to yours. Address yourself to the class and say (in the foreign language, of course):

Tell him to speak louder.

The same technique can be used for other situations where you find the need to give the same command over and over again. For instance,

Tell her to speak faster.
Tell him to hurry up.
Tell him to pay attention.
Tell him to stop speaking to his neighbor.

If you want to make it more personal you can insert the student's name in the above statements.

Teach a list of classroom expressions in the foreign language and use them constantly. Such commands as "Raise your hand," "Come to the front of the room," "Open your notebooks," "Close your books," "Listen carefully," "Repeat after me," "Sit down," "Stand up," should be understood very early in the course.

6. Do not stand only in front of the room. Walk around occasionally and be sure to get to the far corners of the room. The students who are seated there need to feel that they are not very far away from you and your attention.

If you have movable furniture arrange it so that the students face each other. If the class is small arrange the chairs in a circle. If the class is larger keep a center aisle down the middle of the room and place two or three rows of chairs on either side of the aisle facing each other. These arrangements are better for dialogues and conversations than the traditional "one row behind the other" seating plan. It is more natural to be facing the one to whom you are speaking than to be looking at the back of his head. Furthermore, students can hear and understand each other better when they can see each other's faces.

7. Do not teach with a book or notebook in your hands. To refer constantly to your book may give the impression that you do not have a very good command of your subject. Use 3 x 5 cards described above under Item 3. When you need information, glance at the card quickly and unobtrusively. Make the language you use in teaching appear to be as spontaneous as possible. Furthermore, the 3 x 5 cards allow you to use your hands and arms readily for gesturing and motioning.

8. A fast, lively, warm-up drill on some aspect of pronunciation is one good way to start a lesson. It brings the class together quickly and it motivates the student to be careful of his pronunciation for the rest of the class period. It also provides a constant review of the phenomena of pronunciation.

9. A record which presents a selection as the class is entering the room can become a regular pre-class activity which adds several minutes to each period. An assortment of cultural tid-bits can be offered in the five minutes which precede the period, the time which is usually wasted by the students who are waiting for the class to start.

The selections can be musical or spoken and should be repeated several days in a row. They may be properly introduced and identified by the teacher either before or after they have been heard for the first time by the students. Selections of popular or classical music, a short anecdote, speeches by prominent people or excerpts from poetry or plays are interesting to hear. The repertory of offerings may be repeated many times during the semester until they are easily identified by the students.

10. Never leave the assignment of homework to the last minute just before the bell rings. Never give homework page numbers orally without then writing them on the board. Give yourself enough time to explain the assignment and to give a few examples to be sure that everyone understands the problem and knows where to find the exercise.

11. Do not collect written homework without going over it first. It is important that students discover their mistakes while the problem is still fresh in their minds. Do not go over written homework orally. Oral correction cannot show up such potential errors as mistakes in spelling, accents, capital letters, agreement of adjectives, and verb endings (in French).

When correcting homework do not repeat the errors which the students have made; give them the correct form instead. Never write an incorrect form on the board (see page 120).

12. Develop a sensitivity to the mood of your class. Have they learned the item you are teaching? Learn to recognize the symptoms of boredom. It is important not to leave a drill too soon but it is just as important to learn when you have reached the point of diminishing returns. A student who is bored is no longer learning. Change to another kind of drill, not necessarily to another topic. A different type of drill is usually enough to reawaken the student's interest.

13. To verify if you have put your point across, do not call on the slow student first. You will slow down the lesson and frustrate not only the one who does not know the answer but the one who does. Call on the slow student only after he has heard several examples of the answer you want him to imitate.

Never make a student look foolish or stupid in front of his classmates. Help him over the hurdle as quickly as possible and start him on the right road by giving him the answer if necessary.

Take the time and trouble to praise good performance. The slow student as well as the good student loves recognition.

14. Do not ask a question of the entire class if more than one answer is possible and if you have not first given them the answer you expect. Asking a question which may be answered several different ways results in a babel which is indistinguishable and impossible to correct or corroborate. The student who may have a correct answer but one which is different from the one you finally give him may think he has answered incorrectly.

For instance, there are several possible answers to the question, "What kind of weather do we have today?" One might say "sunny," "windy," "cool," "good," or "beautiful." All of these are right. To ask this question of the whole class and accept only one or two answers is confusing to the student who may have answered differently but correctly.

15. Control the attention of every member of your class every minute of your lesson. You must feel that they are together and with you all the time. Do not permit your attention to be taken away from the class as a whole for any length of time.

During a lesson do not address yourself to one student alone even if he asks you a question. If the answer is important, will be instructive and is worth the time, give it to the entire class. If the problem is special to the student who is inquiring, and will take too much of your time and attention without benefitting the rest of the class, ask the student to see you alone after class. Very often students' questions will be answered in the course of the lesson anyhow.

If you are correcting one student, address your remarks to the whole class as well as to him. If it is a question of pronunciation have the student repeat after you once or twice, then ask the class in chorus to model the sound for him. Have him repeat it once again after the chorus.

If it is a question of structure, do not wait too long for the correct answer. You may ask another student to give the correct form or you may give it yourself. However, once the form is given always call upon the class to repeat and model the correct structure. This keeps them together, involved in the correction, and under your control. Go back to the student after the choral repetition and have him repeat the correct form.

It is when one student diverts your attention for a long time that the class "falls apart." Students become restless and talkative if they see that what you are involved in does not concern them. If this should happen a lively, snappy choral repetition will help to pull your class together again.

16. When a question of spelling or form is raised either by you or a student write it on the board so that it can be seen by all. Do not spell it orally and assume that the student and the class will know how to write it.

17. Do not allow yourself to get side-tracked. Be sure to get the answer to *your* question before you answer any other question which might be asked by a student.

18. Ask the question before indicating who is to answer it. You want everyone to think about the answer and not just the one student who is going to answer it. Do not call on a student by name but point to him. You slow yourself down when you pronounce students' names after each question. Furthermore, when you point, each student must look at you or else he will not know if it is his turn to answer. You will surely keep your students' attention if you look one way and point the other.

19. Do not announce that the topic which you are about to teach is going to be difficult. If you do, you start out by giving yourself a handicap. The insecure student may give up before he begins.

20. Do not practice too many forms at one time. Drill one until it is learned before going on to the next one. Do not leave a drill until you have put to use the structure you have taught. Ask questions which will necessitate the use of the structure in the answer.

21. Get acquainted with the new machines and equipment. Start with a simple one like a filmstrip projector. Practice using it by yourself first, away from students and other members of your department. Familiarize yourself with it thoroughly before you attempt to use it in class. Only by learning to use the machine will you be able to know its potential and what you can expect to do with it in your teaching. Even though you may not run the

machines in class yourself you must know how they function before you ask someone else to run them for you.

22. Do not try to operate the machines and teach at the same time. Entrust the operation of the machines to some of your students and leave yourself free to teach. Do not always call on the same student; you will find that many students know how to operate the new equipment and will be very flattered to be given that responsibility.

23. Do not use materials or equipment which are not in perfect working order. For instance, if the movable hands of the clock do not stay in place, it is better to use one which you draw on the board. Anything which does not perform perfectly in front of your students causes you consternation and results in disorder in your class.

24. Rehearse your presentation. Prepare and arrange the materials you intend to use in your lesson ahead of time. Arrange the flash cards, pictures, and other illustrative materials in the order you are going to use them. To riffle through stacks of materials in the middle of a presentation looking for an illustration is distracting to the student, interferes with the train of thought you are seeking to establish and, moreover, cuts into the time you have for teaching.

ON IMPLEMENTING THE TRADITIONAL
TRANSLATION-GRAMMAR TEXTBOOK

Following are some of the ways in which the traditional textbook can be used and implemented to meet the needs of that teacher who does not want to discard the book but who wants nonetheless to incorporate in his teaching some of the new techniques. Many of the suggestions listed below can be carried out by the teacher alone in his classroom. Some of the changes may involve departmental decisions and the cooperative effort of several teachers working together.

The Reading Selection

1. If there is a reading selection at the beginning of the chapter it can be treated orally first, with books closed, using some of

the pre-reading techniques described in Chapter 4. Following that, some of the reading procedures described in Chapter 7 can be used with books open.

2. The selection which is too long for comfortable oral treatment should be divided into adequate parts. Each part should be taught separately. When the several sections have been taught, summaries or narratives can be required to see if the students have understood the whole selection.

Speaking Practice

1. Use as many as possible of the items in the textbook for basic material upon which to build oral practice. The questions on the reading selection which appear in the book can be used (along with the answers which you supply) for question-and-answer drills (see page 43). If the book does not provide enough questions, add some of your own. These questions and answers may also be used for directed dialogues and chain drills (see page 45).

2. Wherever possible, all structures can be presented first as pattern drills, followed by oral application of the structure (see page 52).

3. All homework exercises can be done orally first before being assigned for further study at home. This not only insures more correct homework but it gives the student the chance to hear the language before he sees it written. Homework correction can also always include oral practice for the class and student (see page 121).

4. Free conversation (see page 40) and culminating projects (see page 48) based on the subject matter contained in the chapter can easily become integral parts of the course of study.

Vocabulary Lists

1. Never present words in lists. Introduce the new vocabulary with books closed using the words in sentences. There are several ways of getting meaning across to the student without resorting to the English translations which appear in the book.

Some obvious methods are the use of pictures, gestures, drama-
tizations, pointing, and real objects.

2. Using words in patterns not only helps the student to comprehend but also the repetition helps him remember the word. For
instance, if you want to teach the meaning of the word "slowly,"
present it in several contexts and act each one out:

I read slowly.
I walk slowly.
I chew slowly, etc.

You may give five or six examples to be sure that the students understand the meaning of the word "slowly." To test their
comprehension give them a command in which they are asked to
do something slowly. Follow it up by asking the student to describe what he is doing.

3. Another way to present the vocabulary in context is by
contrasting two items. For example, if you want to teach the verb
"to open," present it in patterns which contrast two actions:

I open the door, I do not close the door, I open the door.
I open the book, I do not close the book, I open the book, etc.

Using five or six such examples with exaggerated actions
and emphasis will make the meaning of "open" become clear.
Test the comprehension by asking the students to open something. Follow this up by asking the student to tell what he is doing.

4. Even though the textbook lists the English translations
alongside of the foreign words, do not review vocabulary by asking for the English meaning. Use the devices suggested in Chapter 9 on vocabulary testing for the study and review of the vocabulary of any lesson in the textbook.

Grammar

1. Traditional texts usually present several grammatical items
in one chapter. In order to teach your students to use this unrelated material, treat one grammatical point at a time and develop

it thoroughly. Introduce each one orally first by pattern drills. Let the students come to the generalizations before they see the rules in the textbooks. Follow this up by the procedures suggested in Chapter 5 on pattern drills before going on to the next item.

2. Usually the text gives the rule for each syntactical item and follows it by only one example. The same procedure applies to each exception to the rule. Reinforce each grammatical point and exception by adding at least five more of your own examples to the one in the book.

3. If the text mentions an interesting structural or idiomatic phenomenon in passing, develop it yourself by a complete pattern drill and many examples. For instance, the text makes a statement: "than" is translated by *que* before a noun or pronoun, but before a numeral it is translated by *de*. Do not assume that the student will grasp the meaning and will know how to use these two important syntactical technicalities merely by reading a statement about them in the book. Only after *que* has been taught first, followed by a separate presentation and drill for *de* should the two elements be mixed in one exercise.

4. If you desire to avoid all translation from one language to another you may omit those exercises in your text. The rewriting of exercises is not usually a task to be undertaken by a single teacher, although it can be done.

Exercises which give the English word and require the student to fill in the blanks with a foreign equivalent can be replaced by those which ask the student to make a choice from among several foreign words. For instance: Instead of a sentence like:

> (eat) Many people ——— meat.

where the word "eat" is written in English and the rest of the sentence is written in the foreign language, the sentence as well as the choices can be all in the foreign language.

> Many people ——— meat   (wear)
> (write)
> (eat)

5. Cued narratives or compositions can be substituted for themes or compositions where the textbook requires the student to translate from English.

6. The rewritten exercises can be mimeographed in sufficient quantities, properly labelled, and filed to serve the teacher for several semesters.

Supplementary Materials

1. If the textbook is not culturally oriented, the use of authentic audio and visual materials will help to make your teaching come alive. There are many commercially-made exercises on tape and records which are easily obtainable. These may be used as aural comprehension exercises to supplement the chapters of the text and can be used as short reading selections after they have been used for listening and understanding.

2. Many traditional textbooks do not contain illustrative material of any kind. Appropriate visual material, projected or non-projected could be added to make the selections more meaningful and more interesting. Such materials can be obtained from numerous sources (see page 139).

3. If the publisher does not supply taped recordings for the textbook, you might be able to have recordings made of the reading selections and some of the drill material which you have written yourself. A nearby college or university can be very useful for supplying the native voices and the recording techniques.

4. Use as many audio and visual materials as you can to supplement the textbook. The addition of colorful photographic material and a variety of voices will help to make a prosaic textbook more interesting and palatable.

TO THE HEAD OF DEPARTMENT

The head of a foreign language department normally must handle the manifold tasks of in-service training, supervision, and administering to the numerous needs of a department. Following are some suggestions to help him in each of these areas:

1. Encourage and urge your teachers to belong to profes-

sional organizations. Make time available so they can attend meetings, institutes, workshops, and other professional gatherings. See to it that it is not always the same teachers who are sent to take part in all of these extramural activities. Rotate the privilege and give as many of your staff as possible the opportunities to come in contact with the leaders and important lecturers, as well as other members of their profession.

2. Try to bring the best thinking in the field to the attention of your staff. A system for circulating the professional literature which comes your way can be established. Signal a particularly good article by noting it on the cover of the publication. Paste a checklist of names on each book, booklet, and pamphlet so that it may reach all the members of your department. You can do this or assign the task to a student aid. All publications should eventually get back to you for filing so that a department professional library of these periodicals and other pertinent literature for use and ready reference by your teachers can be established.

Along with the professional printed materials, keep in your office the audio and visual materials which you want your teachers to use. Such materials are likely to be forgotten and unused if they are kept in the school library or in the audio-visual center. Your student aid can help you to keep track of these materials, too.

3. Teachers acquire many valuable and new ideas by watching other teachers in action. Intramural visitation should be encouraged as well as visits to other schools. You may want to set up your own classes as demonstration situations, open to all members of your department any time they desire to observe you. In this way you will have the opportunity to show classroom techniques to your staff.

If your school does not make provision for visitation to other schools, try to convince your administration of the importance of such contacts. If your school does permit absences for the purpose of observing other teachers in action, bring it to the attention of the members of your staff and urge them to take advantage of these opportunities.

4. Departmental meetings should be used for in-service training as well as for the usual routine department business.

These occasions can be used for recounting what was seen and heard in other schools and for sharing new ideas. Since doing is much more effective than discussing, the teachers can play the role of the students in the class while the new techniques are being demonstrated to them.

The departmental meeting can be devoted to book reports or discussion of the contents of the articles in the periodicals which are circulating in the department. Some conferences can be set aside for the evaluation and examination of new materials.

Do not permit a salesman to become the professor of methodology for your staff. Draw the lines of distinction between the salesman who is selling you a course and the professor of education who is teaching your staff methods which apply in all situations.

On the Management of the Language Laboratory

Getting the maximum use out of the language laboratory is one of the responsibilities of the head of department. If the laboratory is to be used fully, efficiently, and effectively its administration must be organized so that no extra burdens and undue inconveniences are imposed on the teacher. The following suggestions are aimed at relieving the teacher of some of the managerial problems of the laboratory to free him for working with his class.

1. Organize a language laboratory squad. The squad need not consist of language students only. Its members can come from other departments. The electrical and vocational departments can supply students who are interested in and know how to handle mechanical equipment. The squad can maintain the seating plans and can provide a monitor for each laboratory period. This monitor can have several areas of responsibility during the period. One of his most important duties can be the inspection of each listening post before the start of each class to see that it has not been tampered with during the preceding period. If some damage has been done, the fault can easily be traced to the student who used the post last.

The lab monitor can also receive from the previous monitor a list of the posts which are not functioning. It can be his responsibility to get all the students to posts which are in working order and to give the teacher the new seating plan. A very reliable squad captain can be put in charge of contacting the maintenance and repair service at the end of the day and indicating which posts need attention.

A good, reliable, responsible language laboratory squad can relieve the teacher of the burden of inspection, attendance, reseating, and other similar routine tasks. It can get information immediately, each period, on such things as break-downs, and vandalism to the head of department. In schools where these squads perform well, damage to equipment has been reduced dramatically.

A laboratory monitor can also be trained to help the teacher in many other ways during the period. He can be taught to rewind the used tapes and to thread the new ones. He can check to see that the tapes are returned to their proper boxes and replaced in their designated sections on the shelves. He can be trained to splice a tape which breaks.

A laboratory squad can be taught to clean the recording heads, tighten loose screws in head sets, replace worn out nonelectronic parts, and other such tasks. The members can learn to do many useful jobs which will keep the laboratory in good working order.

Instead of closing the laboratory when classes are not using it, the room can be open every period of the school day with the help of a very efficient and responsible monitorial squad. Individual students might be able to come for extra drill and practice during their study or lunch periods if they were supervised and supplied with the materials they require by a laboratory monitor.

To avoid possible damage to the equipment, most departments do not permit students to use pens or pencils in the laboratory. During the pre-reading phase of language learning, the prohibition of the use of these instruments does not detract from the efficacy of the laboratory. Later on, however, writing may be necessary for more successful learning. The student might profit more from reinforcing the exercise by underlining or filling in words or writing out phrases or structure than from just listening. To prohibit them from writing at a time when it would fortify their listening and learning is to drastically curtail the efficiency of the laboratory. A good squad can make the laboratory much more useful. Under the ever watchful eyes of a monitor, the facilities could be used for every function they are capable of providing.

2. A weekly departmental laboratory schedule is often preferable to a fixed schedule for the semester. The weekly schedule permits the teacher to sign up for laboratory time whenever he decides that the lesson requires drill and practice. A schedule set up for half periods is a good way to expand the use of the language laboratory. The teacher need not spend a whole period in the laboratory if he does not think it is necessary. This procedure gives the schedule more flexibility and can accommodate more classes during the week. With a weekly, sign-up schedule no teacher feels forced to take his class to the laboratory at a time when neither he nor his class is ready for it.

3. Do not limit yourself to the use of tape. There are many very good records on the market which you should add to your collection of laboratory materials.

4. Before asking a teacher to record tapes for the laboratory ask yourself several questions:

a. How well does this teacher command the foreign language? Does he have a native or near-native accent? If his performance is mediocre the department will not benefit from any tape he produces.

b. Have you imposed this task on a teacher who has a full day's teaching load? If you have added this taxing job to all his other responsibilities he will probably not be able to do his very best work for you in any of his tasks.

c. How much does this teacher know about recording, timing, editing, scriptwriting, and the many other intricacies involved in producing good tapes? If he is not familiar with even one of these techniques the results of his efforts are not likely to be of good or acceptable quality. The tapes in the library should be of the highest quality possible.

d. Are there commercially-made tapes which are available? If there are you will save a considerable amount of teacher's time and effort and acquire much better materials if you buy them instead of making your own.

APPENDIX B
FOR PROFESSIONAL REFERENCE

National Foreign Language Associations:
American Association of Teachers of French
  Information Bureau
    972 Fifth Ave.
      New York, N.Y. 10021
American Association of Teachers of German
  Service Bureau
    Colgate University
      Hamilton, N.Y. 13346
American Association of Teachers of Italian
  Information Bureau
    Gonzaga University
      Spokane, Wash.
American Association of Teachers of Spanish and Portuguese
  Wichita State University
    Wichita, Kans. 67208
American Association of Teachers of Slavic and East European Languages
  Department of Slavic Languages
    Brandeis University
      Waltham, Mass.
The Modern Language Association of America
  4 Washington Place
    New York, N.Y. 10003

Professional Periodicals About Foreign Language Instruction:
American-German Review
  Carl Schurz Memorial Foundation
    339 Walnut St.
      Philadelphia, Pa. 19106

The DFL Bulletin
  Department of Foreign Languages
  NEA
    1201 Sixteenth St., N.W.
    Washington, D.C. 20036

The French Review
  A publication of the American Association of Teachers of French
  (see above)

The German Quarterly
  A publication of the American Association of Teachers of German
  (see above)

Hispania
  A publication of the American Association of Teachers of Spanish
  and Portuguese
  (see above)

Italica
  A publication of the American Association of Teachers of Italian
  (see above)

Language Learning: A Journal of Applied Linguistics
  3038 North University Building
  Ann Arbor, Mich. 48104

The Modern Language Journal
  13149 Cannes Drive
  St. Louis, Mo. 63141

PMLA
  A publication of the Modern Language Association of America
  (see above)

The Slavic and East European Journal
  A publication of the American Association of Teachers of Slavic and
  East European Languages
  (see above)

MLAbstracts
  California State College
  Fullerton, Calif.

The Linguistic Reporter
  Center for Applied Linguistics of the
    Modern Language Association of America
      1755 Massachusetts Ave., N.W.
      Washington, D.C. 20036

Information Services of Foreign Governments in the United States:
Brazilian Government Trade Bureau
   511 Fifth Ave.
      New York, N.Y. 10017
Canadian Information Bureau
   680 Fifth Ave.
      New York, N.Y. 10019
French Cultural Services
   972 Fifth Ave.
      New York, N.Y. 10021
Cultural Division of the Federal Republic of Germany
   460 Park Ave.
      New York, N.Y. 10022
Royal Greek Embassy Press and Information Service
   120 East 56th St.
      New York, N.Y. 10022
Guide to Foreign Information Sources
   Foreign Commerce Department
      Chamber of Commerce of the United States
         1615 H St. N.W.
            Washington, D. C. 20003
Israel Information Office
   11 East 70 St.
      New York, N.Y. 10021
Italian Information Center
   686 Park Ave.
      New York, N.Y. 10021
Mexican Government Tourist Department
   630 Fifth Ave.
      New York, N.Y. 10020
Pan American Union
   17th and Constitution Ave., N.W.
      Washington, D.C. 20037

INDEX